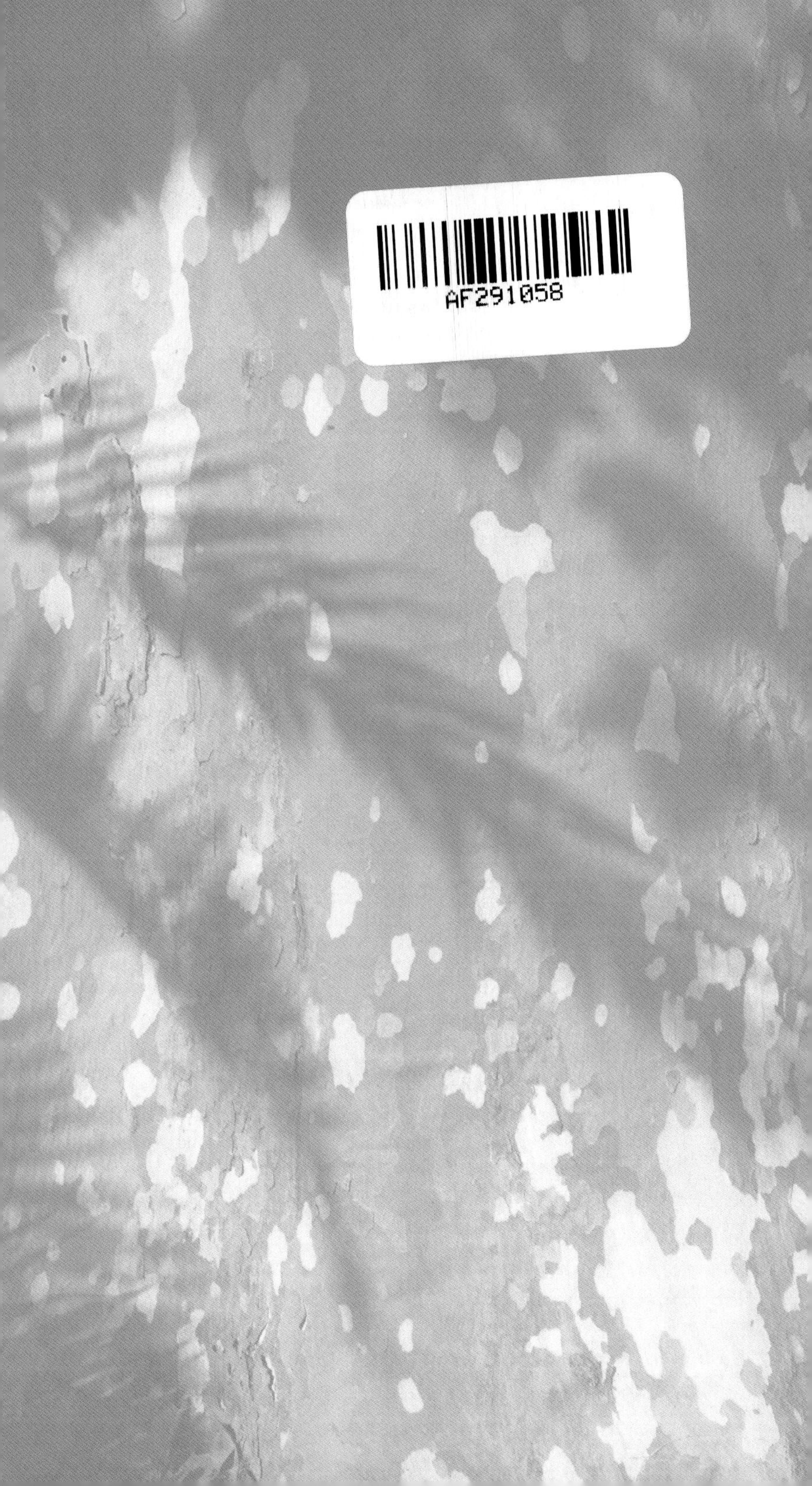
AF291058

# A TREE GROWS *in* QUEENS

*Magali Duzant*

To the tree stewards and gardeners
of the world, both near and far.

# LET ME SING TO YOU NOW, ABOUT HOW PEOPLE TURN INTO OTHER THINGS.

—OVID'S *METAMORPHOSES*

**CONTENTS**

# THE RIGHT FIT

*Flowering Dogwood*

CORNUS FLORIDA

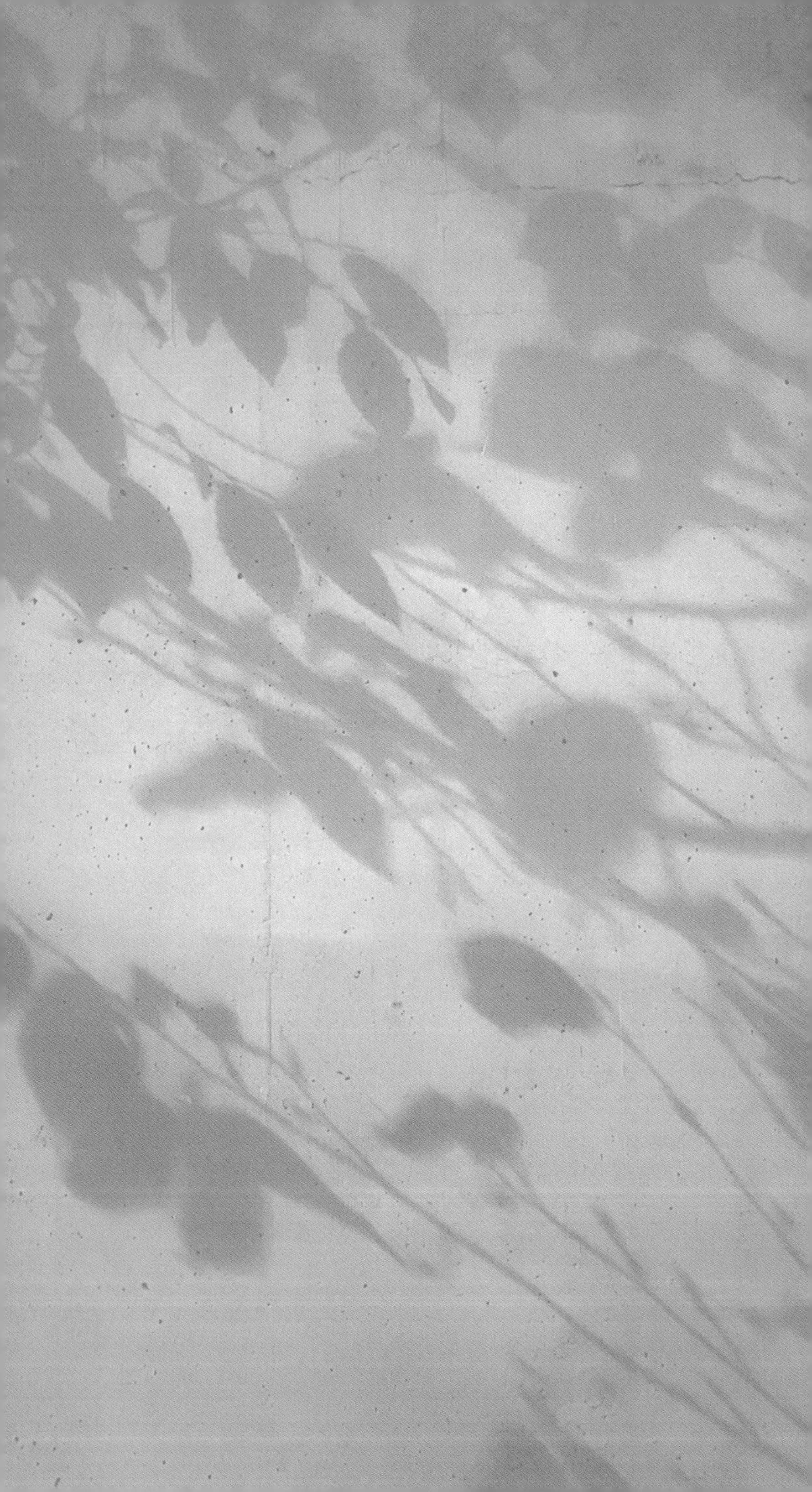

When my mother was young, she and her sisters decided to surprise their mother with a gift for her garden. My grandmother Joan is well known for her obliviousness. She once wore her shoes on the wrong feet for an entire day, not realizing it until she returned from work, complaining that her feet were killing her after the walk from the subway. In my family, when someone does something silly, something without thinking, we say, in a bemused tone filled with love, "Oh Joooaaaannn." This is how her daughters managed to sneak a small tree into their family station wagon on a trip to a nursery and get it home without her noticing.

On Mother's Day, they led her into the garden, where a small flowering dogwood had been planted in the night.

The tree had pink cross-shaped flowers and was by all accounts a lovely addition to the yard.

One morning, several years after the tree was planted, my mother went out into the yard and found the dogwood missing, simply uprooted and disappeared. My grandfather later admitted that he had dug it up and replanted it in Forest Park. The story is strange, and I can't tell if it came out of a fight, some form of excessive revenge, or marital malice. In his later years, my grandfather would sometimes say that he and my grandmother just weren't the right fit. I imagine him silently digging up the tree, driving it to the park, and … replanting it? In my mind this must have taken place at night, much like the original planting; it forms a perfect loop of nocturnal gardening. There is something absurd in how this act of anger and hurt was tinged with just that extra bit of practicality, a result of a Depression-era childhood in an immigrant household that profoundly shaped his ideas on thrift and waste and touched so much of what my grandfather did.

No matter how hard I have tried to find the tree, hiking in and out of trails in Forest Park, I have never managed to find it. The dogwoods I find are always white. Deep down I know how improbable it is that fifty years later I could find a particular tree I had never actually seen, planted somewhere within the forest. But it's nice to imagine that one day I'll turn and see it, a scattering of pink-tipped flowers amid the wash of greens. A tree with a second life, a tree that might have finally found its right fit.

# THE FOSSIL TREE

*Ginkgo*

GINKGO BILOBA

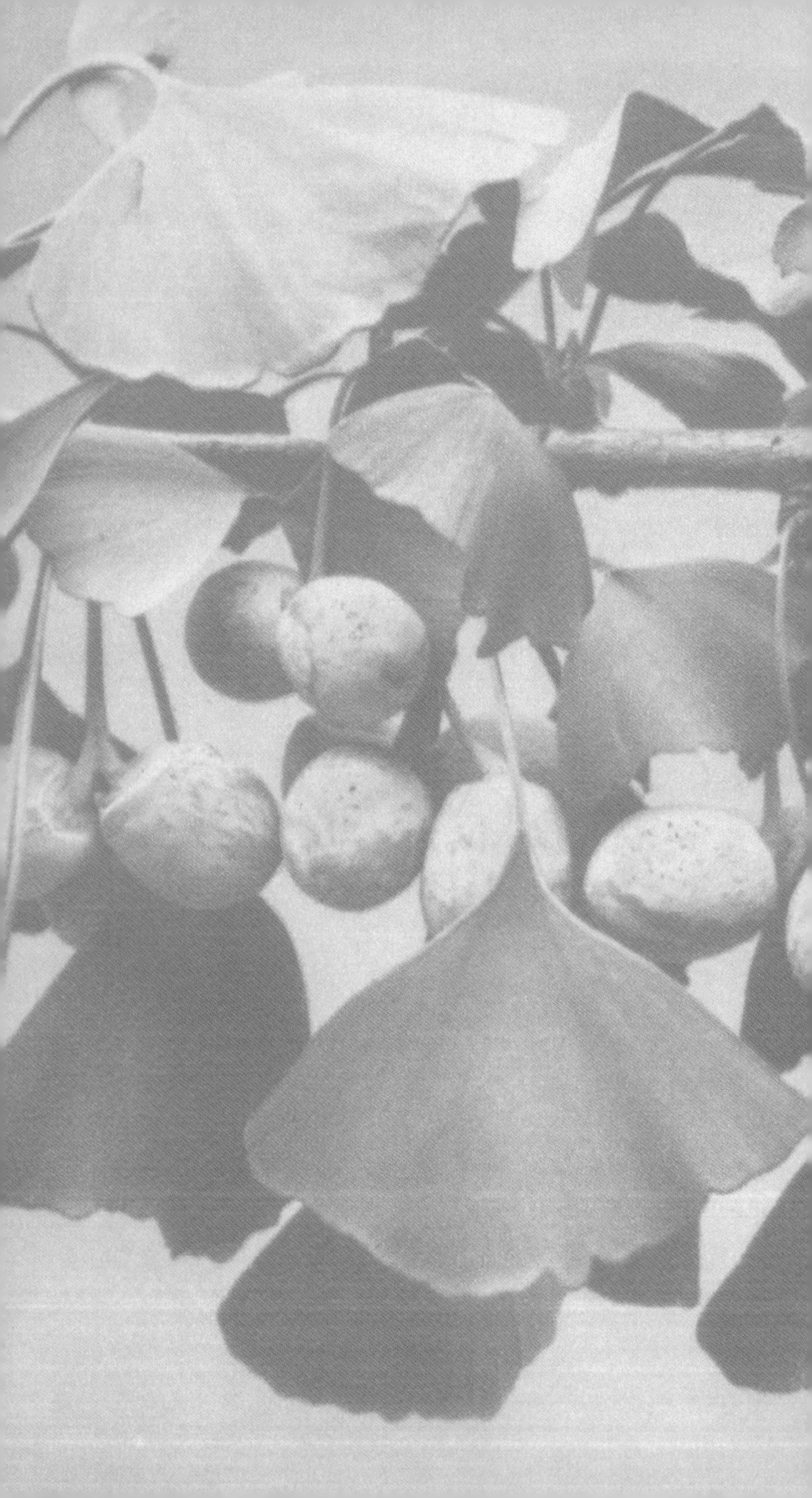

On Fifth Avenue in Manhattan, there is a plaque dedicated to Dorothy Shaver, the former president of Lord & Taylor, one of the city's oldest department stores. In 1945, she was the first female head of a multimillion-dollar firm and a proponent of Salute to Seasons, a beautification program in New York City. In Shaver's memory, the Albert and Mary Lasker Foundation planted twenty ginkgo trees along Fifth Avenue. When I first noticed the plaque, Lord & Taylor had announced its closing. Their flagship store—a 1913 Italian Renaissance Revival structure—had been sold to WeWork, the now-defunct coworking company overshadowed by the exploits of its founder, who then sold it to Amazon. The tree that stood in front of the plaque has since died and been removed; not even a stump remains. Lest this be an overly sad

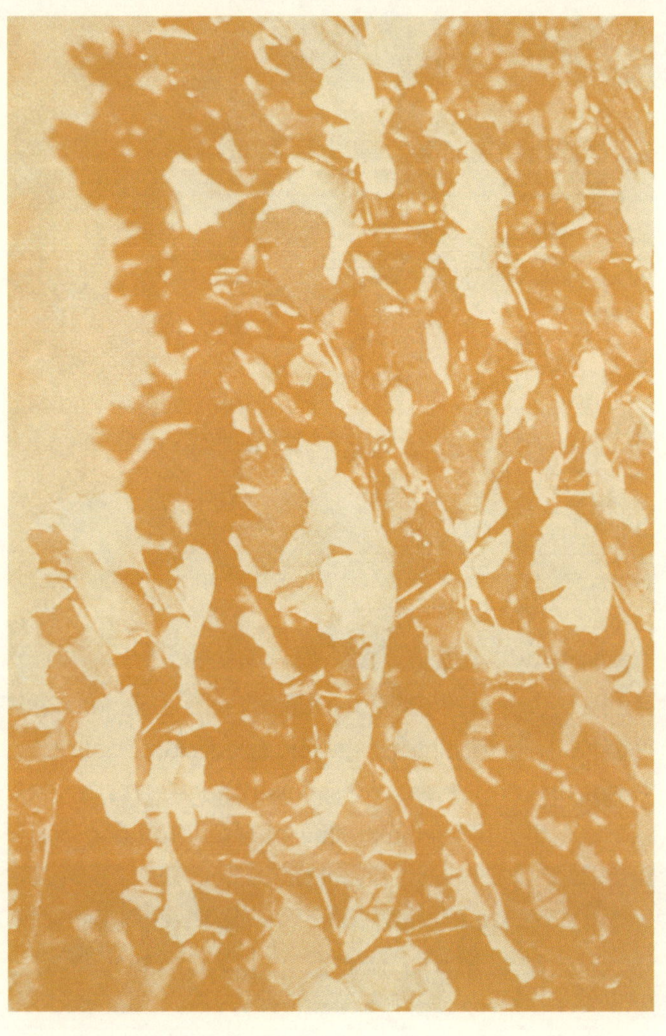

story, it is worth pointing out that most of the remaining ginkgoes have survived, because the ginkgo, if anything, is a survivor.

∽

The ginkgo is a living fossil, said to have coexisted with the dinosaurs. With few relatives, it is one of the only trees to exist in two separate sexes. Ginkgoes are often regarded as originating from Asia, which is true—they did. However, if you reach back as far as one can, you will find that the ginkgo—or the fossil tree, as it is sometimes called—was native to the landmass Pangaea. When the supercontinent broke apart, the ginkgo landed in Asia, where it thrived as a hardy tree known for its longevity—some are more than a millennium old. In 1784, the ginkgo first arrived in the United States by way of a Philadelphia-based botanical collector. Just over a century later, the architect Frank Lloyd Wright developed a love for the fan-shaped leaves and encouraged planting ginkgoes in cities across the country. In Manhattan, ginkgoes make up roughly 10 percent of all street trees; they can thrive in polluted air and have few, if any, pests.

In autumn, the ginkgo's transition to yellow splendor makes its alternate name, maidenhair, ring true. If you've seen a ginkgo, you may have also smelled a ginkgo—the female trees are known for the distinct odor of their seeds; some say vomit comes close to a description. The first superintendent of the United States Botanic Garden noted in 1895, "The ginkgo, or maidenhair tree, is one of the very best; it is first class. The only objection

is the bad odor the fruit has when matured. My first handling of it cost me three hours' time and a bar of soap to
be rid of it."

§

The ginkgo tree has had one of the most surprising jour-
neys, far more than the arc of a glamorous department
store building ending up in the efficient hands of Jeff
Bezos. The tree in front of the Dorothy Shaver plaque
may be gone, like Lord & Taylor in its midcentury glory,
but I find comfort in the notion that perhaps the trees
that survived were female, greeting their new Amazon
neighbors with a show of color and a rancid hello.

# TO LIVE FOREVER

*Oak*
QUERCUS

*Linden*
TILIA

*Cypress*
CUPRESSUS

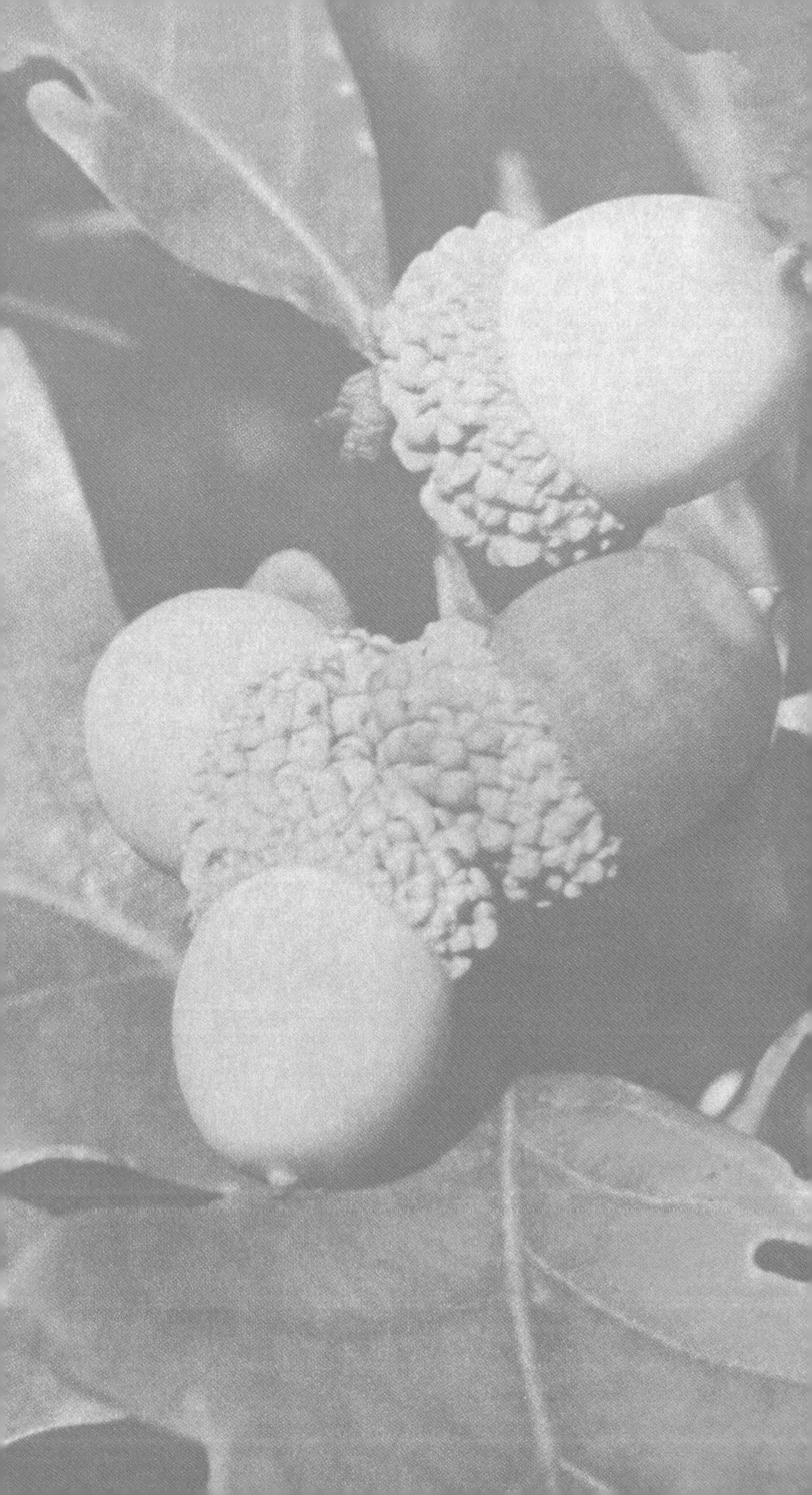

The modern English word *tree* can be traced back to the ancient Greek word δρῦς—pronounced "drys"—meaning "oak" or "timber." This root is shared by the modern words *duration, endure, durable*. Our contemporary word for "tree" comes from the Old English *treo, treow*, and *triewe*; the latter meaning "faithful, trustworthy, and honest." A tree, enduring, ever faithful, always true.

In his epic narrative *Metamorphoses*, the Roman poet Ovid recounts the myth of Cyparissus, a young companion of the god Apollo. One day while hunting in the woods, Cyparissus accidentally killed his pet stag with a misguided arrow as the animal lay sleeping. Overcome by grief, he begged Apollo to let his tears fall forever. Obliging, Apollo turned him into a cypress tree, whose

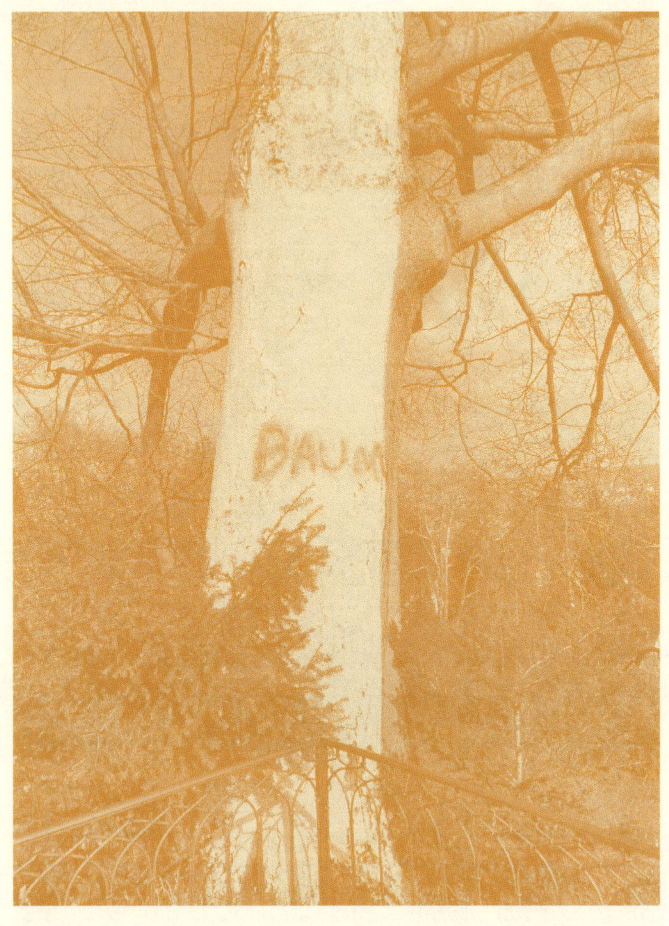


1    *Baum* is the word for "tree" in German.

sap dripped in tear-like beads. In another myth, an elderly couple, Baucis and Philemon, were the only mortals to open their door to strangers in need. Unbeknownst to them, the strangers were gods disguised as wanderers. In reward for their generosity, the gods granted them the power to live on as trees after their mortal deaths. Thus, Baucis and Philemon became living monuments to grace and kindness—an oak and a linden, respectively.

The neighborhood around the Jefferson Market Library in Greenwich Village is a veritable arbor of tree memorials. One day, sitting on the back steps of the library, I noticed a dusty plaque with a small dedication tucked neatly in the dirt beneath a young maple tree. It read: "In memory of Harry Baum,[1] who loved and restored life for so many, 1920–1998."

Nearby on West Ninth Street, there is a tree plaque dedicated in loving memory to Victor Ramos that reads, "If you want to live forever, plant a tree." When has immortality ever been quite so easy? One day, on a Reddit spiral, I found a picture of the same plaque with a stump. Someone had cleverly and cringingly written, "If you want to live forever, become a meme." The original tree appeared to have been cut down, likely due to tree rot or damage, and at some point the plaque was dedicated to a stump. When a new tree was planted, another plaque was dedicated, another attempt at immortality, perhaps rebirth or reincarnation. A fellow user named bs9tmw tried to clear up the chatter about the stump photo, writing, "I don't think so. Obviously a tree isn't going to live forever; its death was inevitable just like Victor's was. They were going for something deeper, like the tree having given life to many animals, or being the mother of many more trees, or the way the tree affected the lives of all those around it." It's a simple riposte to the trolls; as always, amid the shit bloom moments of beauty. Another commenter replied, "Even funnier is that his name is Portuguese and 'Ramos' means branches. The man was a tree himself!" One of those occasions where the internet can be lovely, the way following a tree from its roots to branches leads you onward and upward, as if breaking through the canopy of a forest, where a welcoming view awaits. Sometimes the key is just to stop scrolling once you find it.

# A TREE BY
# ANY OTHER NAME

*Tulip Poplar*

LIRIODENDRON TULIPIFERA

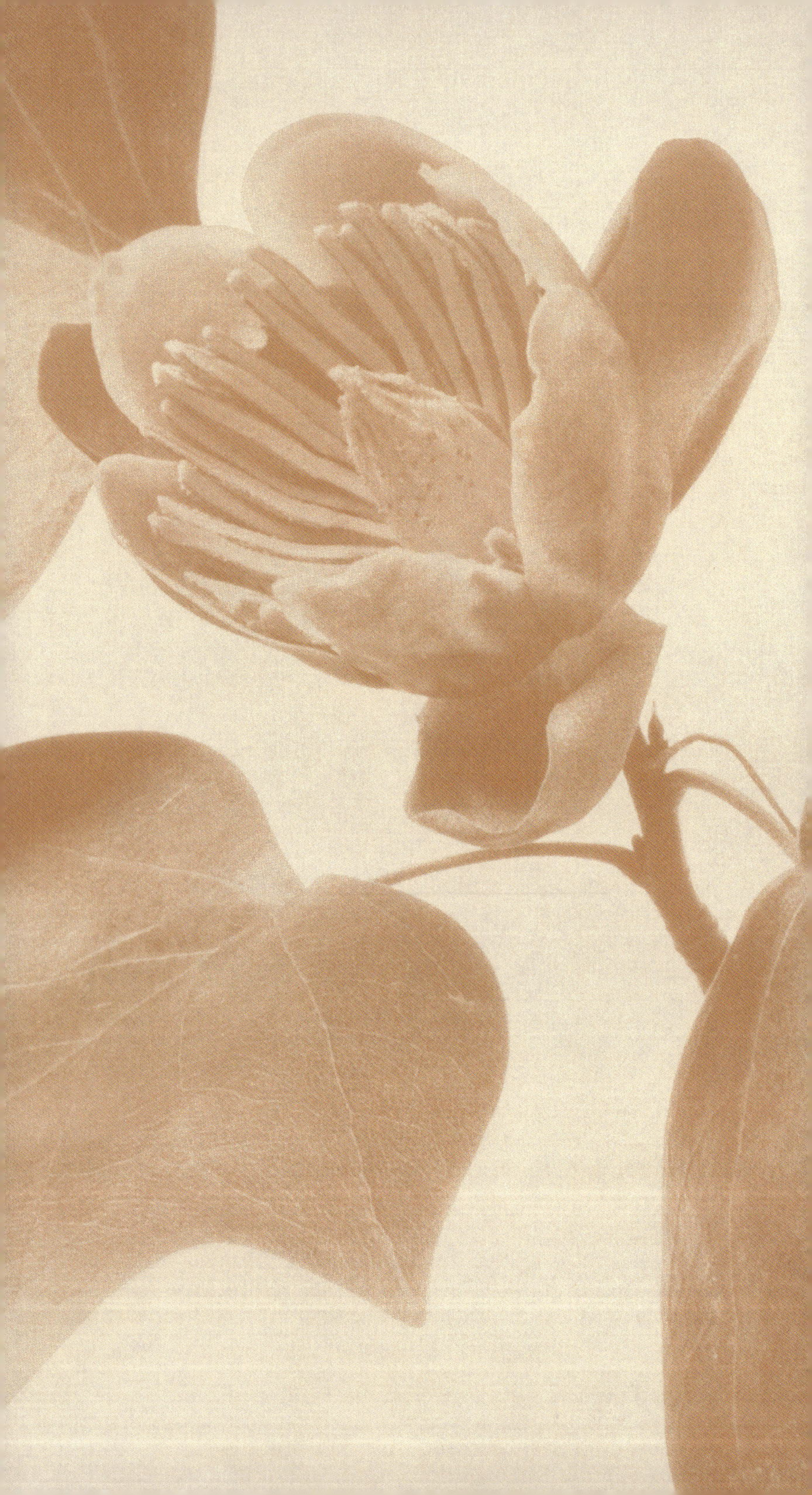

Rooted on Matinecock land, nestled between two parkways, down a ravine and through some poison ivy, is the tallest and oldest tree in New York City. Neither a tulip nor a poplar but a tulip poplar, or *Liriodendron tulipifera,* meaning the no less misguided "lily tree that carries tulips." This Northeast native, nicknamed the Queens Giant, is also known as the Alley Pond Park Giant. In the Miami-Illinois dialect, the species name is *oonseentia;* it was called "canoe tree" by early European colonizers, as Native peoples used it to construct dugout canoes.

The tulip poplar is more closely related to a magnolia tree than to a tulip flower, but its blossoms might cause one to do a double-take. Ranging from yellowish green to orange, they could easily be mistaken for the flower that caused tulipmania—the seventeenth-century speculation bubble in the Dutch Republic, in which prices for tulip bulbs soared and then dramatically bottomed out. The Queens Giant stands in some of the last old-growth forest of the city; it is 133.8 feet (40.8 meters) tall with a 19-foot (5.8 meters) circumference. It is believed to be between 350 and 450 years old, meaning that it has existed since this sliver of land was first colonized by the British. In fact, the tulip poplar was one of the first trees imported from America to England, spurring the start of a furious export of plants that transformed English gardens.

You can't ask the tree, "What is your earliest memory?" Nor can it tell us what it was like when colonizers moved in and the Matinecock were pushed from their land, or when war broke out and George Washington supposedly passed through the forest, or when houses started being built, or when tar was poured and cars started streaming through belching exhaust, creating a consistent low din of traffic. But in visiting the tree, you might start to ask yourself those questions or imagine those scenarios, because down in the ravine away from the parkway, you realize that time stands still.

To get to the tree, you first need to get to the park. There is no subway that is truly close, so a bus is your best bet. The trail to get there runs along the expressway; a sparse line of trees separates the path from cars. At some point it turns inward, and the foliage becomes lusher, weedier, fecund. In spring, the wisteria had started to bloom, splashes of pale lilac on green neon against the dull white

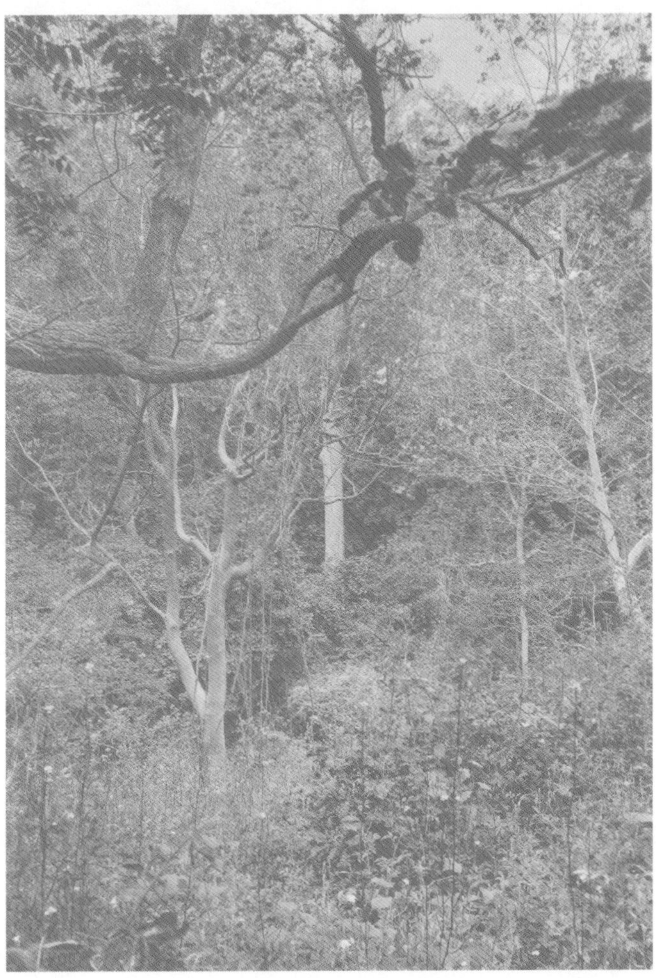

of the sky. It is easy to miss the Giant, as at first it looks like any other tree. We passed the overgrown trail, retraced our steps, looked for a marker, but found nothing. And then, it was suddenly obvious. The tree did not appear to be much bigger than those surrounding it, and yet it somehow stood apart. The trunk seemed to stretch for ages, a silvery gray amid the green. To get to the base of the tree, we slid down a path or what we thought was a path, sidestepping poison ivy, the forest floor soft from all the rotting leaves. Standing in front of the tree, I had hoped to feel some kind of awe, of history; but the tulip poplar doesn't hold the same reverence as a giant redwood or a sequoia. The Queens Giant was simply another tree—large, with a hollow in its base and a rickety black chain-link fence around it. This lack of awe is most likely why it is as old as it is. The ordinariness of it all becomes a layer of protection. The New York City Department of Parks and Recreation has communicated their policy toward the tree as one of benign neglect. If the tree isn't a tourist destination, it can grow old in peace, or whatever peace can be found a few hundred yards from an expressway. That said, the Queens Giant rates 4.9 out of 5 stars on Google; no wait time or reservation needed.

# TROPICAL TRANSPLANTS

*Palm Tree*

ARECACEAE

*Sweet Orange*

CITRUS SINENSIS

Walking is the best way to see New York City: as you move through the city, block by block, certain patterns begin to emerge—Starbucks stores, CVS pharmacies, Citibanks, $1 Pizza places, halal carts, and fruit stands. Near my home, the closest fruit stand is parked outside of a now-dormant Duane Reade pharmacy (soon to be CVS), next to a Starbucks and diagonal from a Citibank. Year-round, through heat and cold, you can buy apples, oranges, bananas, broccoli, cucumbers, and other produce from farther afield. There is an office chair for the vendor that, once the cart closes up shop around midnight, gets chained to a spindly honey locust tree.

One day, on the way to the train, I noticed a box on the lowest shelf overflowing with small, hard-shelled green

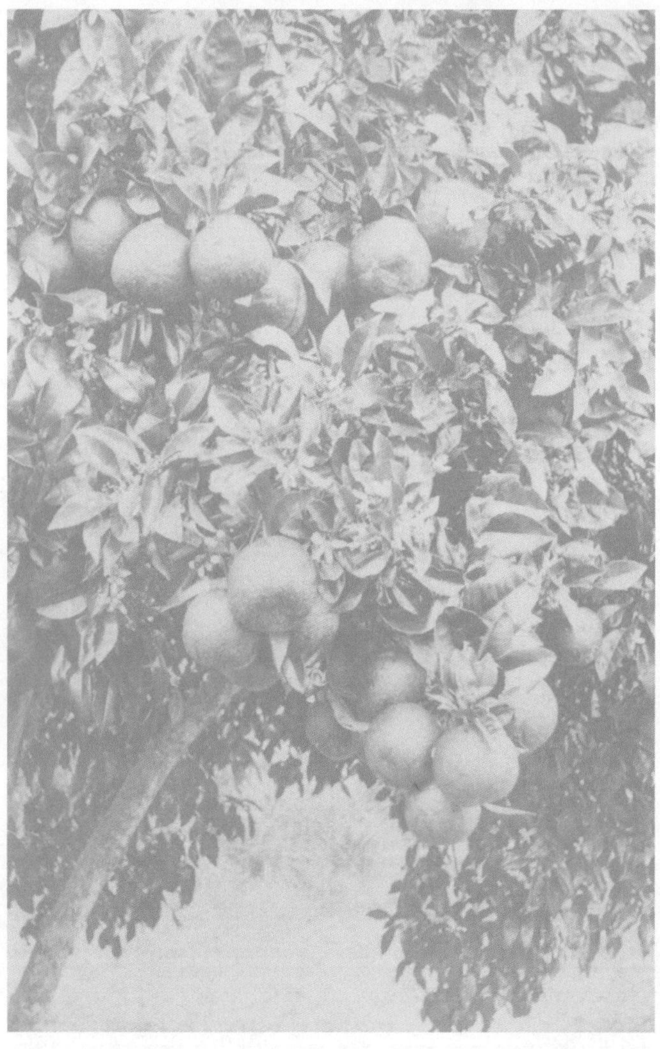

(∗) On a lazy Sunday while frittering away the time, I came across
an article that seemed to answer my question. In 2019, New York
state's first new town in over three decades was created. It is called
Palm Tree, located in Orange County, and grew from a zoning conflict
between the town of Monroe and the village of Kiryas Joel—which
itself was originally created as a retreat for a Satmar community of
Hasidim led by Grand Rebbe Joel Teitelbaum. So, in a sense, maybe
you can grow a palm tree in New York.

fruits on a branch, a few leaves scattered throughout, placed next to fuzzy brown coconuts. I was instantly transported to a memory of my father, under a huge quenepa tree outside my grandmother's seafoam-green bakery in the Caribbean. To eat a quenepa, you must bite through the shell first; a quick crunch will split it in two, revealing a pale-orange almost melon-like fruit around a hard white pit. My father would reach up into the tree and pull down a branch of fruit. On other occasions, he would shimmy up a short palm tree outside the pink concrete house to cut down a coconut or two, letting them fall to the ground, where he would cut off the tops and pour alcohol directly into them. The coconuts had a dull thud and a bit of a bounce when they reached the ground.

I know that a coconut cannot truly grow in the city, but I still find myself searching Google for other nonnative fruit trees in Queens.[*] While walking, you might see a miniature lemon tree for sale or a fig tree in a private garden. In the nineteenth century, Italian immigrants would dig trenches, partially sever some of the root system, and bend their fig trees to bury them so that the trees could overwinter in the cold months. It is now warm enough in the area to no longer have to do this; often an insulated plastic blanket will do. My grandmother has a small orange tree that gets wheeled out into the yard in the warm weather; it bore sour fruit in two separate blooms this summer. During the 1939–1940 and 1964–1965 World's Fairs, tropical trees and plants grew in Queens in stunning numbers. In preparation for the 1939 World's Fair, the ash heaps of Flushing made way for over ten thousand trees within the space of a year, while orange trees were brought up from Florida alongside a variety of palms. For the 1964 World's Fair, the Hawaiian pavilion put a field of pineapple bushes on display with a sign reading "Do Not Pick or Eat Fruit."

∽

It is often said that you can find anything you desire in New York City, but that might be more a saying than a reality—I don't think you can truly grow a coconut tree. Tropical trees might not grow in the city naturally, but I think of all the other transplants like my father who sought out a bit of home in a potted tree or at a fruit cart triangulated between dollar slices, Frappuccinos, and drugstores.

# EARLY SPRING

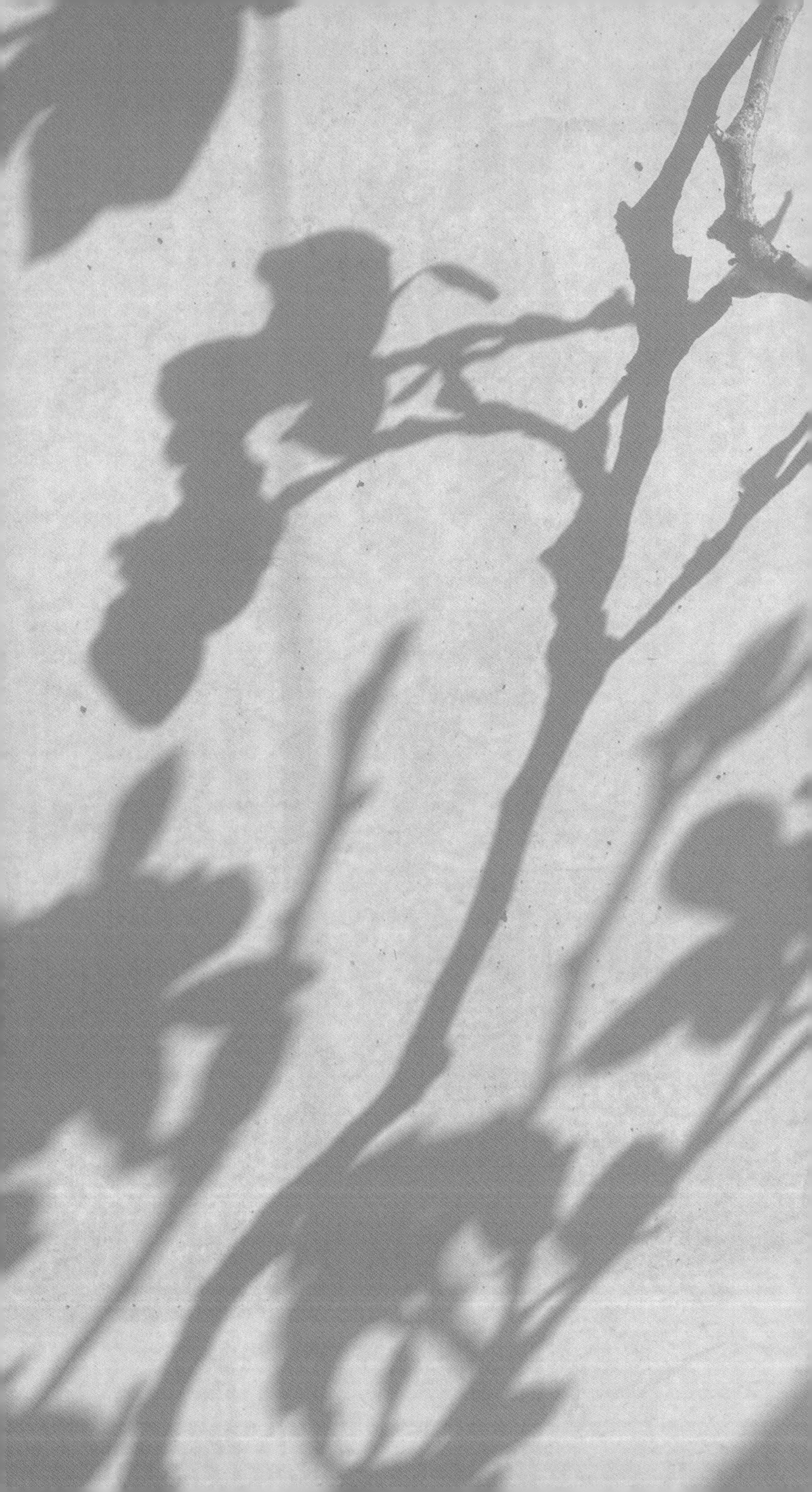

One sticky, sweaty summer night at a rooftop gathering in Brooklyn, I mentioned that I grew up in a New York City apartment without air-conditioning. The effect was akin to having said I'd been following someone named Q and believed in lizard people, which I do not; but I did spend more than twenty-five years in the city with little more than a fan. I got used to the fact that summer evenings were just miserable; though, as the years pass, it does get harder.

೬

New York City, according to the Köppen climate classification, has had a humid continental climate for as long as these measurements have been taken, but times change and the city is now moving into the humid subtropical zone. The worldwide average or "normal" temperatures have increased by 1.8°F (1°C) since 1900, with a clear acceleration in the most recent decades. We are racing, or perhaps more fittingly sleepwalking—can you sleep-race?—toward what the United Nations has called a "code red for humanity."

By 2040, New York City is projected to move from the USDA Plant Hardiness Zone 7 into the warmer Zone 8. Take a walk through the city, and you may notice camellias, native to the American South, in full flower. Out for a stroll, I came across one, split down the middle, creamy white blossoms on one side, fuchsia on the other. Crape myrtles, native to Southeast Asia and parts of the South Pacific, with their shaggy pink and lavender flowers, are growing larger and larger, while cherry and magnolia trees are blooming in late March instead of April. In fact, as I write this in February at my desk in Zürich, dozens of lopped-off magnolia branches lean against our neighbor's house with a note to *bitte mitzunehmen*—inviting passersby to help themselves to a branch, full of buds and ready to bloom.

One of the things that made the first COVID lockdown a bit more manageable was the early spring in New York. There is a fleeting novelty to warmer seasons and evolving floral varieties, but it also means that trees long native to the area, such as the sugar maple, are struggling to adapt to warmer winters and may be on their way out of the city. It seems that spotted lanternflies, emerald ash borers, and other invasive species are consistently on the verge of decimating native plants. The Amazon rainforest is often cited as the lungs of our planet, but what about the lungs of our cities? Urban landscapes contain a kind of forest of their own; street trees line avenues, parks, medians, and even stretches of true forest. These urban forests provide much on their own, from beauty to health and relief, a relief that is often connected to one's socioeconomic status. In a recent heat dome phenomenon over the Pacific Northwest, temperatures broke records for days on end, at one point reaching 116°F (46°C) in Portland, Oregon, on a day when an average temperature would have been 73°F (22°C). Within these unprecedented temperatures there were giant disparities; in

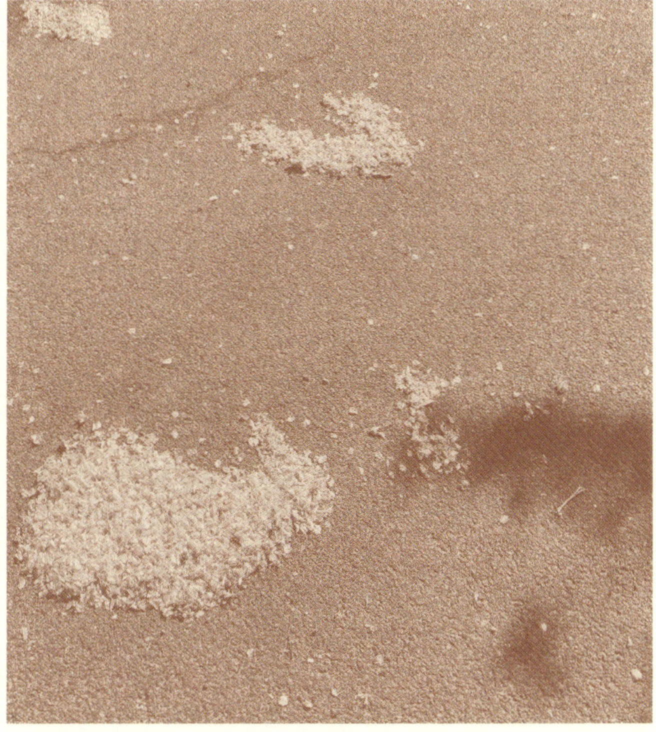

lower-income neighborhoods, shaped by redlining and destructive urban planning policies, where tree cover is sparse, the temperature of blacktop was as high as 180°F (82°C). Meanwhile, in wealthier areas with abundant trees, the blacktop only reached 99°F (37°C).

Trees present an equity question—a recent study showed that older Black New Yorkers are twice as likely to die during an extreme heat event as white residents. Trees help combat urban heat islands, which form from a combination of black asphalt, lack of vegetation, and proximity to highways and parking lots—hence the push to plant more trees and to paint rooftops white in cities. In short, trees create shade, which in turn cools the ground and thus the surrounding areas. To reduce carbon levels and reduce warming, the necessity of trees cannot be overstated. And yet, as with most endeavors in a hyper-capitalist society, there is always a way to do the worst while claiming to do the best. Recent studies reveal that many of the corporations claiming to plant trees to offset their carbon emissions are planting the cheapest varieties or those that can be logged later, regardless of biodiversity concerns. More capitalism is never the answer to capitalism's horrors.

〽

As temperatures rise, cities are future-casting what their street trees might look like down the line. Long gone will be the cold-hardy maples and red oaks, but what will the cities of the future look like? Hopefully a bit more like forests and less like the imagined hellscape of lizard people.

# THE FLOATING TREE

*Bay Laurel*

LAURUS NOBILIS

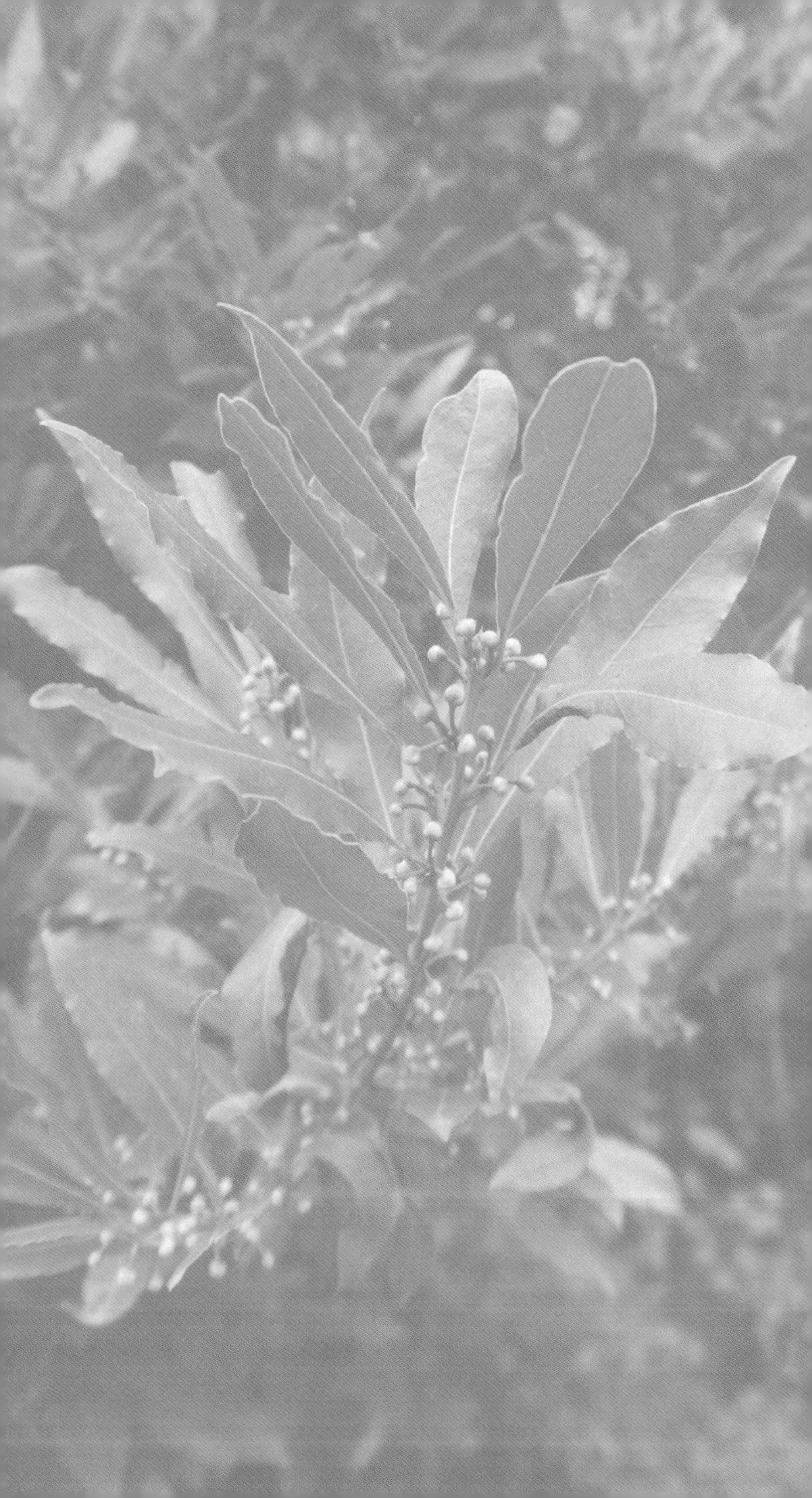

Sitting in the dark of my apartment, I watch a tree float across my computer screen. It is an image of eerie calm, as much a feat of balance and bravado as it is a dreamlike vision. People gather along the side of a road staring, crying, and whispering among themselves before forming a procession behind a towering tree and following it out of town as it wavers on the extra-long flatbed of a truck. The tree's trunk is nearly the width of the road itself; a shot from above shows the rustling and swaying of its leaves as it travels on, as if in reluctant agreement.

In Salomé Jashi's documentary *Taming the Garden*, the Georgian billionaire and former prime minister Bidzina Ivanishvili's obsession with trees creates a series of arresting scenes. In 2020, Ivanishvili opened the Shekvetili

Dendrological Park, situated on the Black Sea coast and featuring winding paths with over two hundred majestic trees that had been uprooted and shipped—literally put on barges and floated across the sea—to be planted in his pleasure garden. Free to the public, the park includes trees that are over one hundred years old. Rumors abound about his continued influence over the government, his potential Druidic interest in the trees and their energy, and his tactics in taking the trees from their communities. The fact remains that there is little that reads as such hubris, such power tripping, as the human greed of bending nature—its branches and roots—to one's own will.

Stories of man submitting nature to his quest for power, avarice, or simply a thrill are as old as time; this type of violence is still alive and well. It is also notably local. In 2023, a "tree killer" rampaged through Greenpoint, Brooklyn, cutting down a crape myrtle, a magnolia, and a honey locust among others. In 2018, in a dispute over solar panels, a former *Top Chef* contestant poisoned a neighbor's seventy-year-old silver maple tree by drilling holes into its trunk and filling them with herbicide. Looking further afield and deeper back in time, one might find that this kind of damage results from twisted forms of desire.

Two thousand years ago, during the height of the Roman Empire, Ovid transcribed the myth of Apollo and Daphne —the Greek word for "laurel"—in *Metamorphoses*, the fifteen-book narrative poem in which he recounts the history of the world through a series of myths and historical events, often with a theme of transformation. Ovid's concern with human agency, power, and fluidity emerges throughout recurring themes of violation; *Metamorphoses* includes at least fifty tales of sexual violence and rape. Speculating about Ovid's literary motives, Stephanie McCarter, the first contemporary female translator of *Metamorphoses*, believes they come from a desire to shock the reader, inviting them to contemplate how power operates. She posits that the overly stylized translations of *Metamorphoses* hide the reality of the acts described: *plunder* and *ravish* replace the word *rape* in early translations. When accused by trolls of writing a feminist translation, McCarter responds, "In terms of translating the sexual violence, I actually think I'm translating the text more accurately."[2]

In Ovid's telling, a nymph runs through the woods, tripping over roots, her arms scratched by branches. She is pursued by Apollo, who, having been struck by Eros's arrow, has fallen in love with her. Out of breath, perhaps out of time, she stops. There is no way out that she can see. She calls out to her father for help, and in return, "[her] prayer spoken, dull weight grips her limbs, as slender bark enfolds her supple torso. Her hair sprouts up as leaves, her arms as branches. A stiff root clasps her foot, just now so swift. The treetop takes her mouth. Just her gleam remains."[3]

To escape Apollo, the nymph, named Daphne, became a laurel tree. In this myth, love would be more accurately described as lust, obsession, and a desire to possess.

While Daphne transforms, Apollo says, "Since you cannot be my wife, you'll be my tree! You will adorn my hair, laurel, and you my lyre, and you my quiver."[4] Daphne never truly escapes: in his claim on her, even if only in tree form, Apollo demonstrates how what we aver to love we can so easily exploit and abuse.

To this day, the laurel tree is associated with Apollo's victory—its pointed dark green leaves are a symbol of achievement. The word *baccalaureate* comes from *bacca lauri*, the berry of the laurel. Most are familiar with a laurel under the guise of its other name, *bay*, as in the dried leaf used the world over and found in many dishes, including Indian biryanis, Filipino adobos, and French stews, or sitting in spice jars on dusty bodega shelves. Winners of the New York City Marathon, after running past countless bodegas in five boroughs, are crowned with a laurel wreath. For what is an achievement if not something procured through effort, cunning, force, or even at times deceit?

2   Stephanie McCarter and Jia Tolentino, "The Brutality of Ovid: A Conversation on Sex, Violence, and Power in the *Metamorphoses*," *Lapham's Quarterly*, September 11, 2019, http://www.laphamsquarterly.org/roundtable/brutality-ovid.

3   Ovid, *Metamorphoses*, trans. Stephanie McCarter (New York: Penguin Books, 2022).

4   Ibid.

# THE HARLEM
# WISHING TREE

*American Elm*

ULMUS AMERICANA

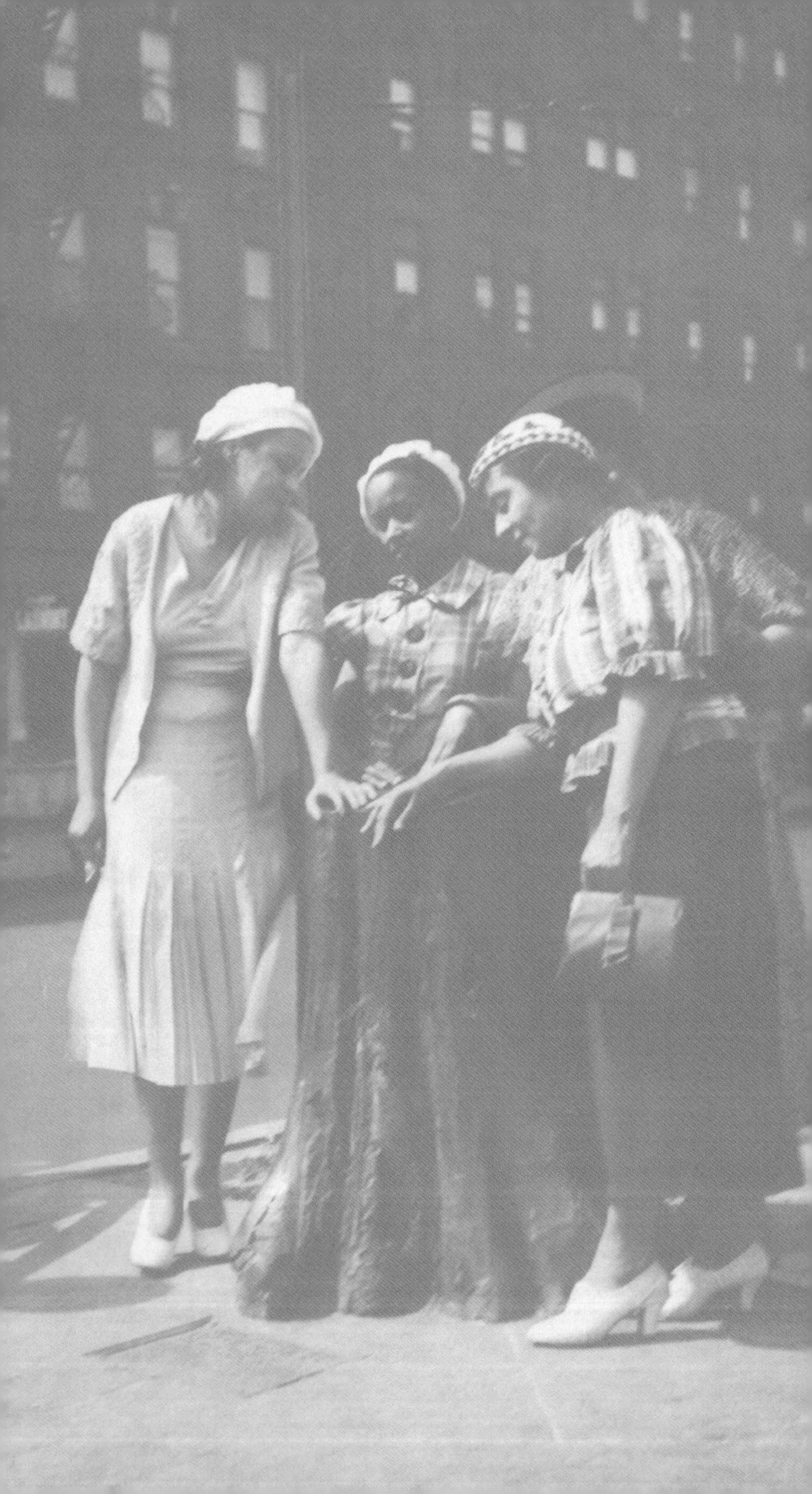

These days, the notion of seeking something out in public to rub or touch seems somewhat horrifying. When the COVID-19 pandemic engulfed the world, a form of ritualistic hygiene emerged. Prior to understanding the aerosol aspect of the virus, experts told us to wash our hands often, wear gloves, and avoid touching surfaces. This led people to hoard hand sanitizer and antiseptic wipes, wash every item they purchased at the bodega, and leave packages in the mail room for days before handling them. But before the pandemic, people purposefully sought out communal surfaces to rub, touch, or, in the unsurprising case of female statues, grope. Tourists worldwide kissed the Blarney Stone; rubbed the arm of Everard t'Serclaes in Brussels or the snout of *Il Porcellino* in Florence; and, because even statues of women can't escape indignities, caressed the breasts of the Juliet statue in Verona or the Molly Malone statue in Dublin (the statue is also called "The Tart with the Cart"). In the 1930s in New York, if one was looking for luck, they might find some in Harlem at the Tree of Hope, also known as the Wishing Tree.

∽

The original tree, an elm, stood on the corner of 132nd Street and Seventh Avenue. Musicians would rub the tree's bark and branches for luck before playing gigs at nearby venues, such as the Lafayette Theater. In 1934, the Parks Department cut the tree down to make way for construction projects. In response, Bill Robinson, the celebrated tap dancer and actor known to many as Bojangles, had the tree's stump—as well as a new young elm—replanted on the traffic island of 131st Street. The replanting ceremony had everything from a marching band and dancers to the city's diminutive mayor, a mascot of sorts, Fiorello La Guardia. The tree stump was commemorated with a plaque and stood there until 1972. When the original Wishing Tree was cut down, its trunk was divided up and auctioned off; a section of it ended up at the Apollo Theater. To this day, performers rub it before stepping out onto the stage, hoping to pick up some luck.

If a tree can bring luck to the hand of the person touching it, can that hand bring something to the tree? It's nice to think that we can have reciprocal relationships with nature. In the 1970s, hands saved a forest of trees and gave birth to the modern concept of tree hugging. The Chipko

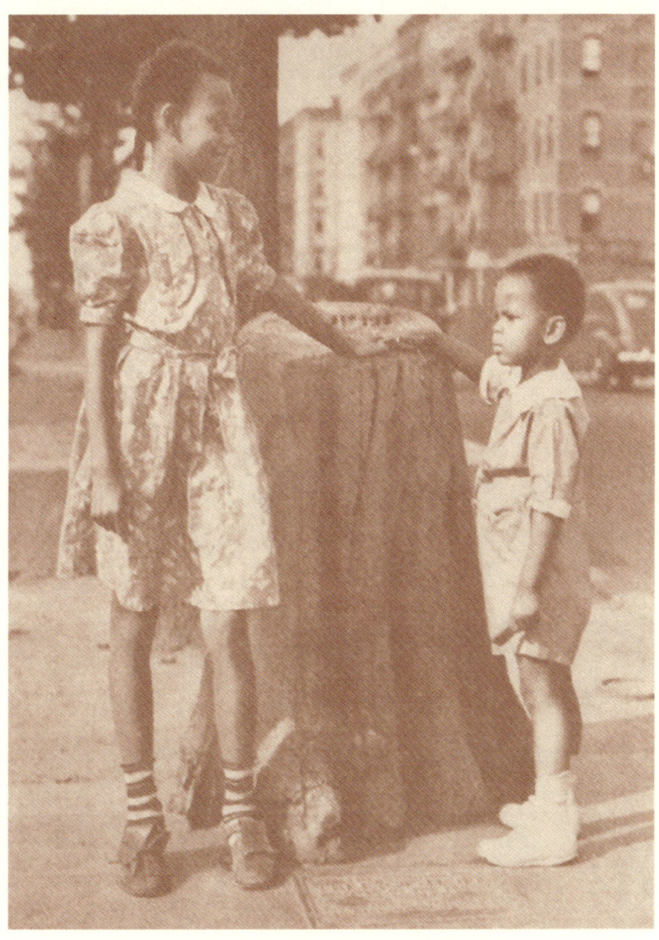

movement (also called the Chipko Andolan movement) was a response to the rapid development experienced by the states of Uttarakhand and Uttar Pradesh. *Chipko* in Hindi means "to cling to or embrace." In 1973, in the village of Mandal, villagers were denied access to a stand of trees; they were planning to use them to build tools, but the stand had been sold to a corporation for logging. In an act of protest, the villagers embraced the trees to prevent

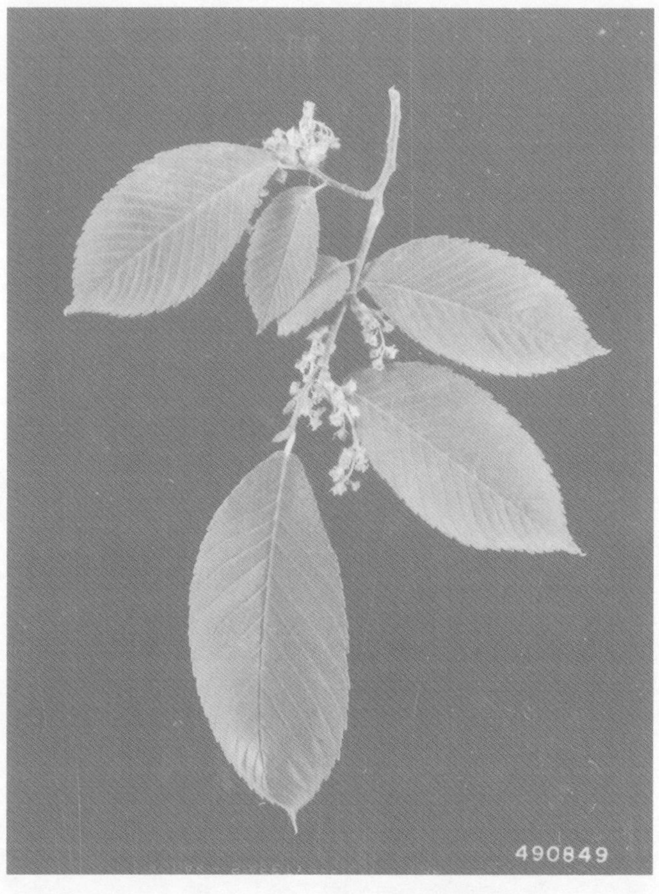
490849

them from being felled. The Indian environmentalist Sunderlal Bahuguna helped spread the movement's tactics throughout the state and coined the slogan "Ecology is permanent economy."

In 1974, the Chipko movement emerged in the village of Reni, when the male inhabitants were invited to a nearby town, most likely to get them out of the area as the forest was cleared. This left the women of the village, led by Gaura Devi, to confront the loggers. The pictures taken that day show women hugging the trees, holding each other's hands to wrap themselves around the trunks, as an unbreakable chain. The ripple effects of the protest actions swept across the Indian state, giving birth to a decentralized movement for forest rights. The villagers understood the reciprocal relationships at stake: yes, the forest was a resource, but one to be treated with care, not exploitation.

In the years that followed the first Chipko action, tree hugging and tree sitting spread beyond India's borders to the forests of New Zealand, Germany, and Northern California, and on to my university campus in Pittsburgh, where a beloved sculpture professor scaled a tree in the nude to protest the slated destruction of it and others for the building of a robotics center. The term *tree hugger* has become a most derogatory remark in wider Western culture, one that is often associated with a white-hippie caricature obscuring the actual history of the movement. In 1730, the first recorded tree-hugging action was carried out by members of a Bishnoi Hindu village; roughly 350 inhabitants sacrificed themselves, murdered for protecting their trees. A royal decree of protection on all other Bishnoi land was introduced—the villagers had given their bodies for their trees.

∽

Touch can be a form of activism. It can be a form of compassion, shared between two organisms, a moment of understanding something larger than oneself. Touch can spark many things, from worldwide movements to small moments of luck.

# A TREE HAS REASON TO CRY

*American Chestnut*

CASTANEA DENTATA

*Weeping Beech*

FAGUS SYLVATICA 'PENDULA'

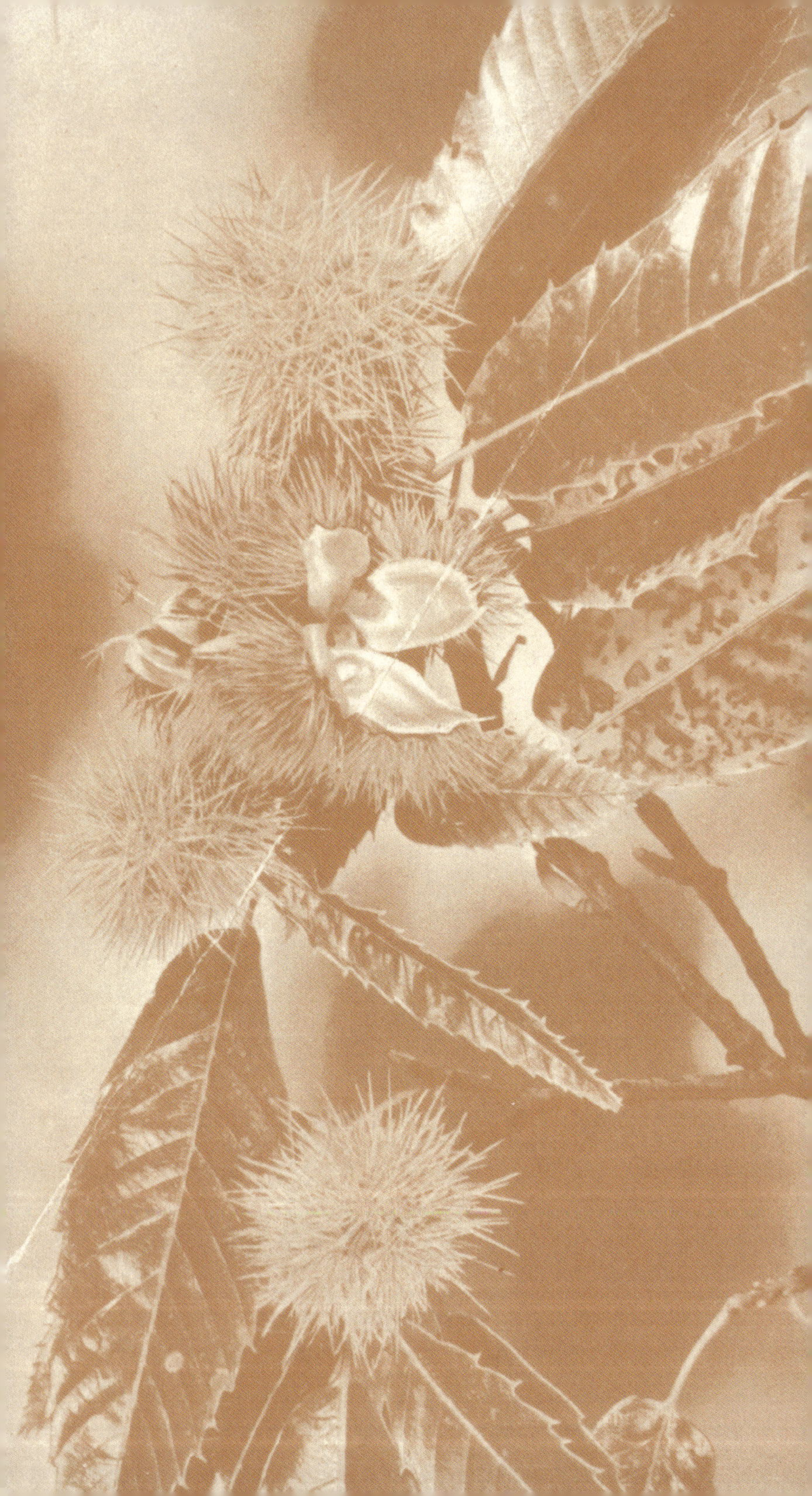

In 1998, a *New York Daily News* headline proclaimed, "Tree has reason to cry." The article announced the death of the country's oldest weeping beech in Flushing, Queens. The tree, considered the mother of nearly all weeping beeches in the United States, was officially declared dead at the ripe old age of 151 by the Parks Department. Planted from a Belgian cutting in 1847 by local horticulturist and nursery owner Samuel Bowne Parsons, the tree had stopped successfully budding. In accordance with its status as a living landmark, a funeral was held, in which attendants were encouraged to hug the tree goodbye. This form of reverence feels fitting, especially in Flushing, home to many of the country's earliest nurseries—the first was opened by Robert Prince in 1737. The Kissena Park Historic Grove stands on the former

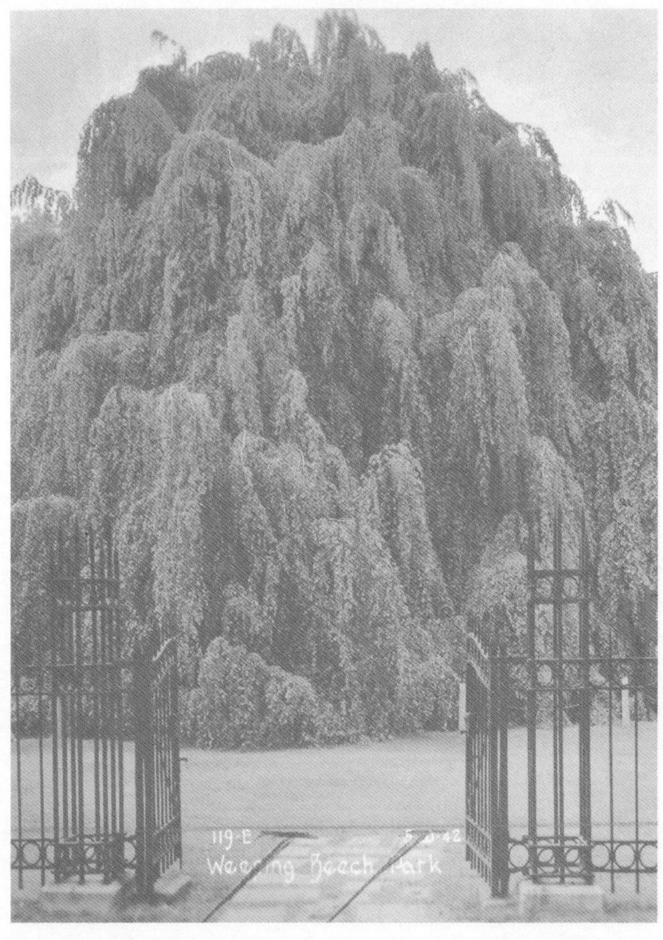


Parsons nursery; the name is taken from a Chippewa word meaning "the cold place" in reference to a nearby lake. Robert Parsons, a fellow nurseryman and brother of Samuel Bowne, once said, "The manner in which Flushingites worshiped the trees practically amounted to idolatry." Trees are like people: they can be overlooked as much as they can inspire great passions; they provide comfort, have growth spurts, get old, fall sick.

In addition to introducing the weeping beeches to the United States, the Parsons family brought the delicate beauty of Japanese maples alongside one of the most devastating cases of tree blight in history. In 1876, Samuel Parsons Jr., a highly respected landscape architect and son of Samuel Bowne Parsons, imported a selection of Japanese chestnut trees. He sold them to customers around the country, unaware that the trees carried the blight-causing fungus *Cryphonectria parasitica*. The trees themselves were blight-resistant, but not their American cousins. In 1904, a stand of chestnut trees at the Bronx Zoo displayed an odd yellow blister-like infection on their bark; by the next year, they were dead. The blight devours the bark and then chokes off the tree's vasculature, preventing the movement of nutrients and water. The American chestnut blight is considered the greatest ecological catastrophe in American history, causing the deaths of over three billion trees. Pre-blight, one in every four trees in the Northeast was a chestnut. They provided shade, a regular nut harvest, and hardy wood used for everything from lumber to railroad ties. The catastrophe was not only ecological but also economic: subsistence farming in Appalachian areas was irrevocably lost, often replaced with dangerous mining operations. In upstate New York, work has been ongoing to attempt to genetically engineer a blight-resistant chestnut, to correct a human mistake.

It's late October, and I am reading about the chestnut blight at a desk in a glass house studio in Umbria, Italy. Billions of trees lost within fifty years—I can neither grasp nor visualize the immensity of this number. The next day, I set out on a walk to a nearby village through the woods. The wind picks up and the sky shifts from blue to gray, the scent of wood smoke is in the air, and the barking and whining of dogs guarding tracts of land echo through the trees. As I turn a corner, I see the chestnuts. They are everywhere, their neon chartreuse burrs piercing the dim forest. A Mitsubishi jeep is pulled up the side of the trail, and an older woman in apron and gloves bends to toss the spiky burrs into a white bucket. Around another bend, three figures in hooded sweatshirts pulled tight collect them on a shaded hillside. The text describing the lost chestnut harvests is playing out in the Italian countryside; buckets are filled, and the discarded burrs scatter the trail. I pick one up without thinking; the bristles sting my hand and I shove it into my pocket. Their abundance feels almost shocking, the impact like a million tiny pricks. I wonder, amid the bounty here, if a funeral was ever held for the American chestnut. How do you mourn a tree?

*Fir Tree*

ABIES

# O TANNENBAUM!

*Fir Tree*

ABIES

On a hot August afternoon, while I sat on the balcony contemplating whether or not to go for a swim, a smudgy orange shape caught my eye. As I turned my head to get a better look, the smudge moved through the air, hurtling three floors down onto the grass below. It was a Christmas tree. Our neighbor appeared a few minutes later, clad in a Hawaiian print shirt. Picking up the tree, she dragged it to the compost, leaving a trail of orange and brown needles in her wake. The previous year, my partner and I picked out a tree early in December—perhaps too early, as it began to droop before Christmas. Walking in the neighborhood, we spotted someone else's discarded tree. It was beautiful and fragrant, as though freshly cut. Later that evening, he went back for the tree. While he biked away from the scene of recycling crime—really

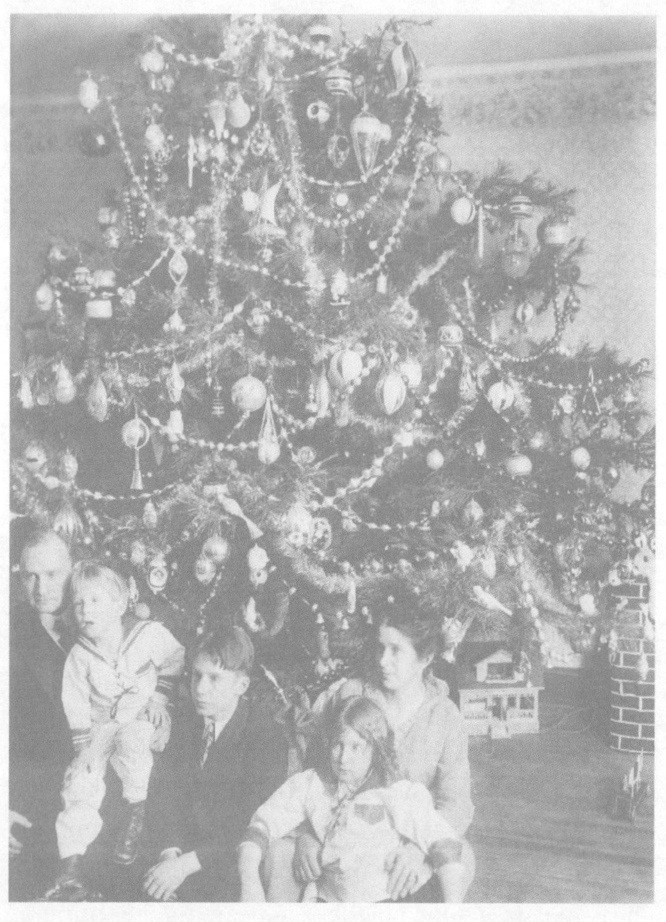

just exercising the second-most-important R of the trio, *reuse*—the tree fell out of the trailer and into the street, illuminated by traffic lights. After he went back on the bike, up the elevator, and into the apartment, we were hanging dried orange slices on our second tree of the season.

∽

There is a magic to Christmas trees, a reason Germans sing about them. As you walk through New York in December, the city's usual smells of garbage, roasting nuts, and urine are replaced by the sharpness of evergreens, fir, and cedar set off by fairy lights, soothing the mania in last-minute shoppers' eyes. There is also a pageantry to Christmas trees, besashed and strung with lights. The sense of spectacle seems to split into three variations: There is the festivity of the countdown leading up to the tree lighting, first done in Rockefeller Center in 1933. There is the fervor of Fox News quacks moaning about the war on Christmas—taking Christ out of that tree even though it turns out he didn't have a ton to do with it to start. And finally there is the social spectacle, perhaps never so perfectly expressed as in the collective outrage toward Rome's official city tree in 2017, nicknamed *Lo Spelacchio*—"the mangy one." A tree that had Charlie Brown's name all over it. It died before the holiday and sparked a corruption investigation.

The modern concept of a Christmas tree dates back to Renaissance-era Germany and the Protestant reform movement. Martin Luther, the last person one might categorize as a romantic, was said to have brought the first tree indoors, adorning it with candles to mimic the beauty of the stars above the forest at night. Queen Victoria and her German husband, Prince Albert, popularized the tradition in Britain, posing alongside a decorated tree for the *London Illustrated News*. The Christmas tree often appeared in mystery plays of the medieval era. Mystery in this sense was akin to miracle; today they would be called living tableaux. In these plays, biblical stories were acted out, sometimes featuring the Paradise tree, a fir adorned with apples and wafers to symbolize sin, redemption, and the Tree of Knowledge from the Garden of Eden. Even earlier connections can be made to pagan festivals associated with the winter solstice. The early Egyptians brought palm fronds inside in the winter months to worship Ra, the sun god. The Romans celebrated Saturnalia, for Saturn the god of agriculture, during the winter solstice. They gave gifts of candles and decorated their homes with wreaths and garlands. The Druids hung evergreen boughs in their temples to celebrate everlasting life; and early Nordic peoples believed that evergreens and hollies could ward off evil spirits, which, if you count seasonal depression as an evil spirit, I'd say still holds true—a bit of color against a winter sky is heartening.

∽

Weeks went by, yet still, I couldn't find it in myself to get rid of our tree. Needles began to appear in the bed, the orange slices fell off as the branches bent, the tree stopped absorbing water, and I absentmindedly flooded the corner it sat in. We discussed how to get rid of it, how to avoid detection and nosy neighbors—to throw it off the balcony or not, that was the question. One night in early April, by cover of darkness, we took the tree down the elevator with a mix of sadness and embarrassment, returning to sweep up the incriminating Hansel and Gretel trail of needles. Easter had gone, the Lord had supposedly arisen, Passover had passed, the crocuses

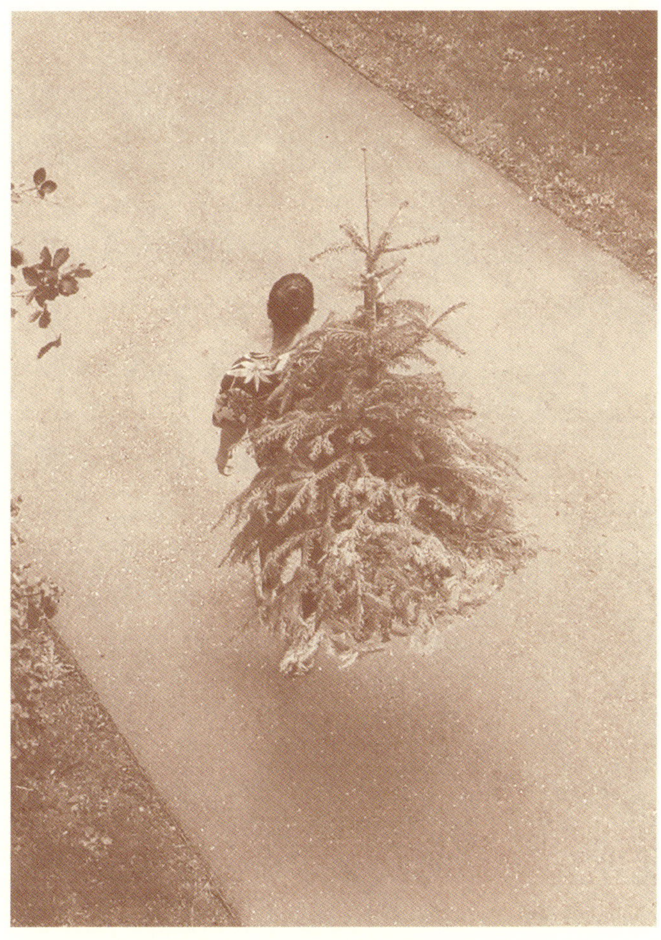

had bloomed, and only then was it time to say goodbye. The tree was loaded into the trailer and biked up into the woods, a final resting place after its multiple incarnations. Dust into dust, ashes to ashes, needles and bark into soil.

# NOT QUITE A TREE

*American Wisteria*

WISTERIA FRUTESCENS

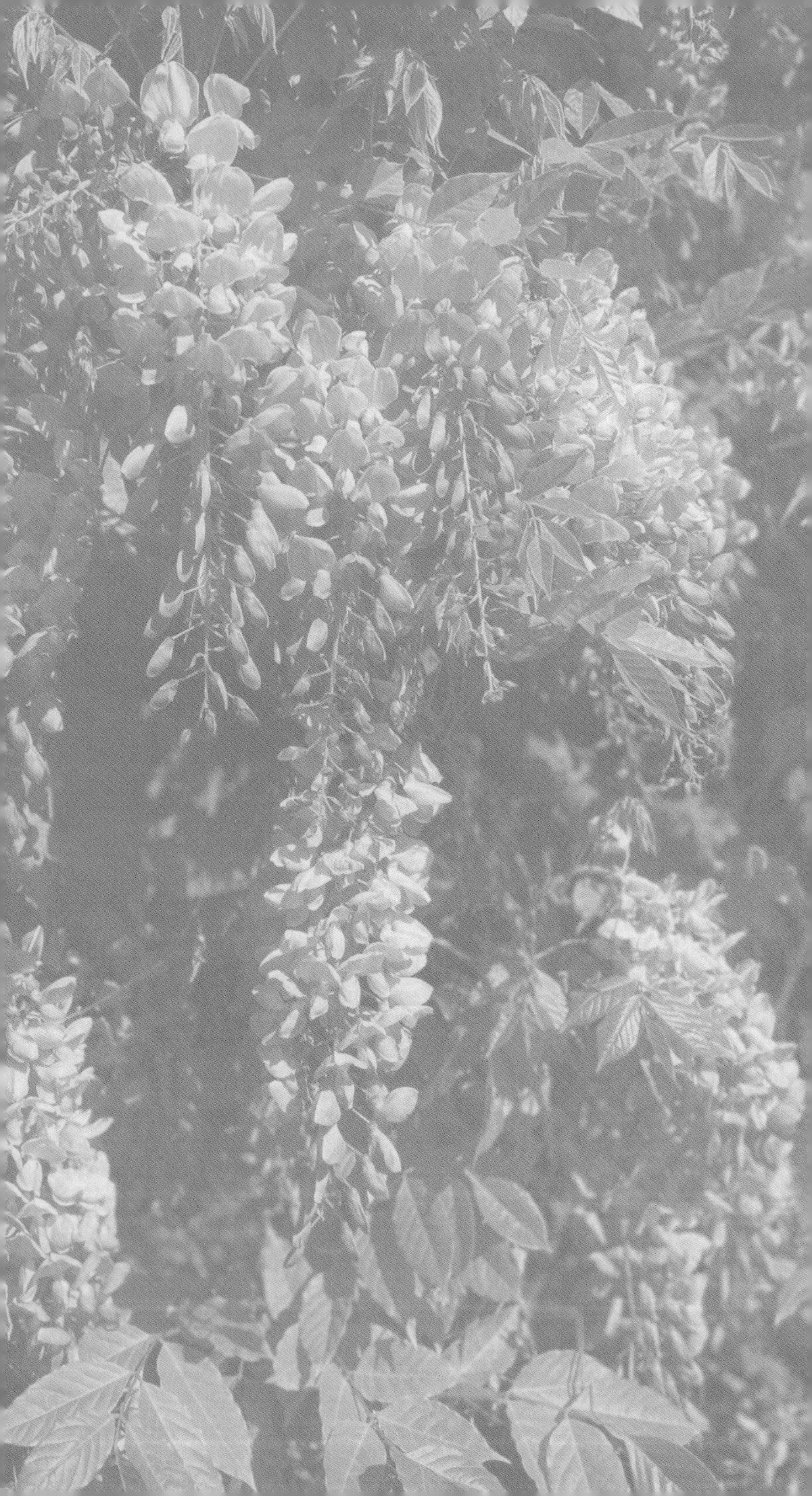

When my grandfather turned ninety, his children threw him a surprise party at a local Turkish restaurant in Forest Hills, Queens. The food was delicious, the wine flowed, the tributes were funny and sweet, and my grandmother may have told us all that they married so young because she was knocked up. A few months later, my grandfather passed away at home, having been able to see and say goodbye to everyone in the family. The last time I spoke to him was on the phone. I told him I loved him, and he said, "Be good, baby."

In the months after his death, something quite lovely happened: the wisteria that grew off the terrace outside of his bedroom and home office began to bloom. It had been years since it had flowered so profusely. We realized that in his illness, his love of pruning had been put on hold; there was no one to hack at the thick vines. The pale purple, almost periwinkle flowers were lush and abundant; they spilled off the terrace and hung down around the front door. Emerging from all the way up the block was a beautiful cloud of soft, trailing strands of violet. As my grandmother observed, the flowers had taken his place.

# A TREE,
# A GARDEN

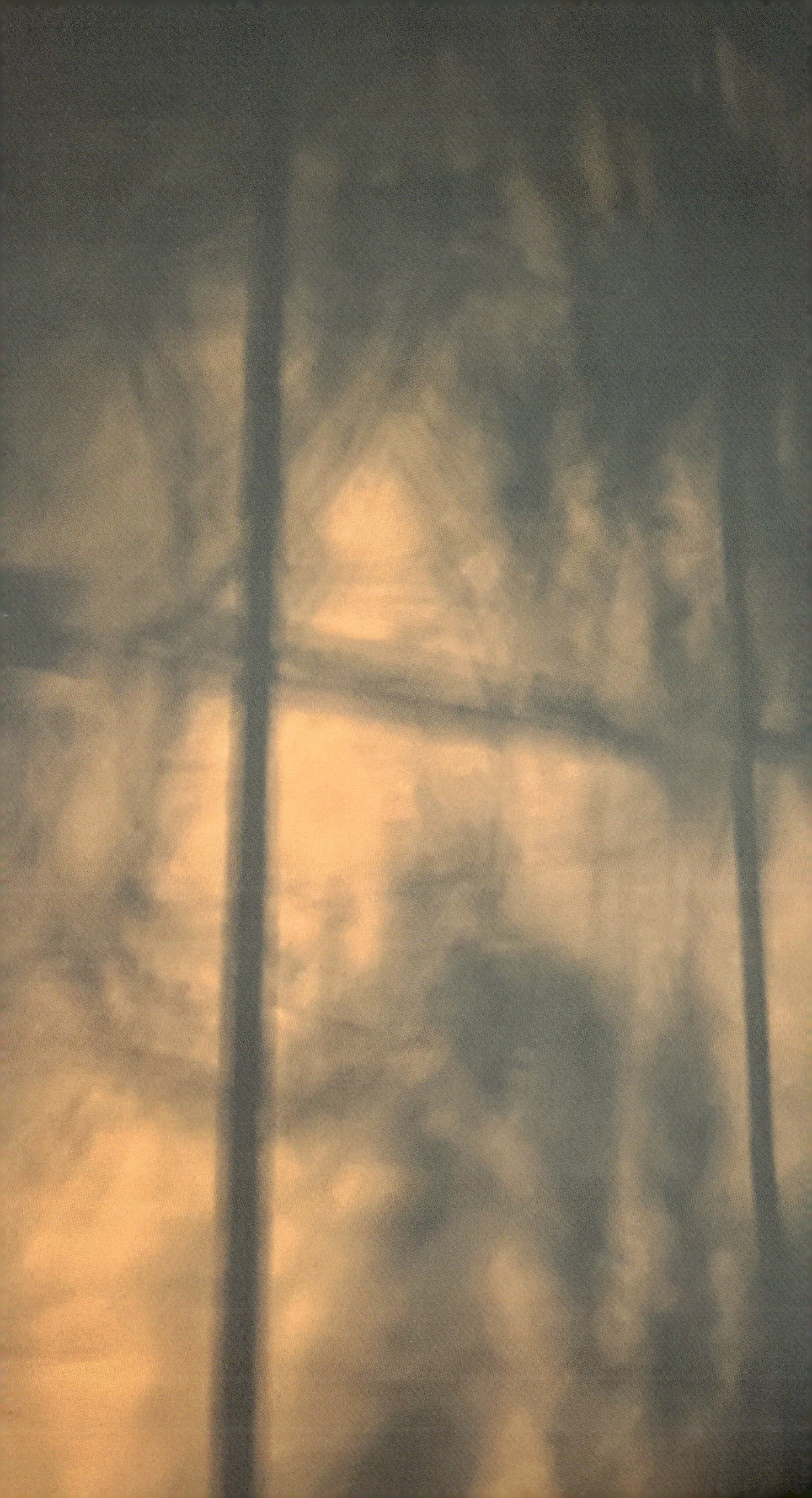

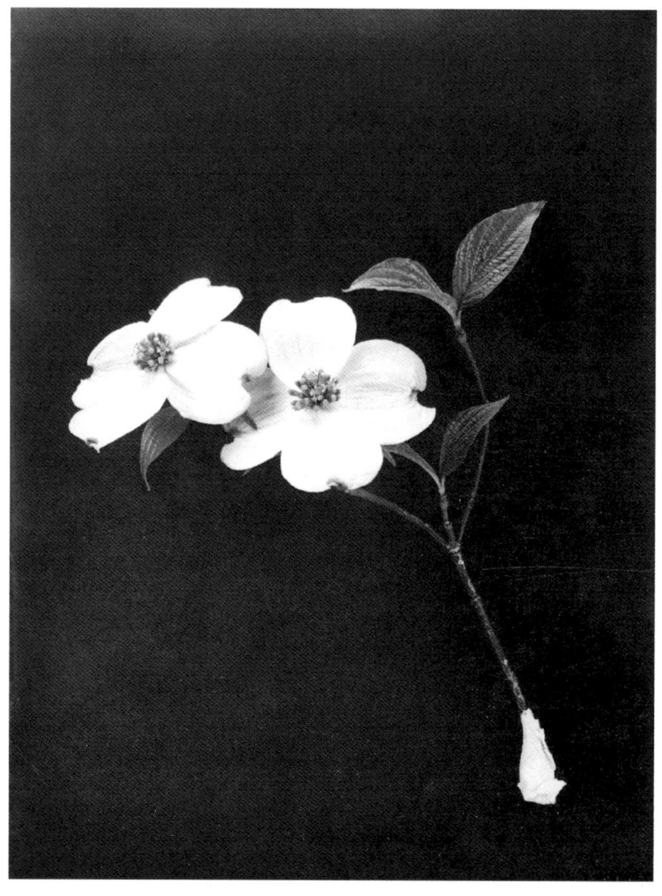

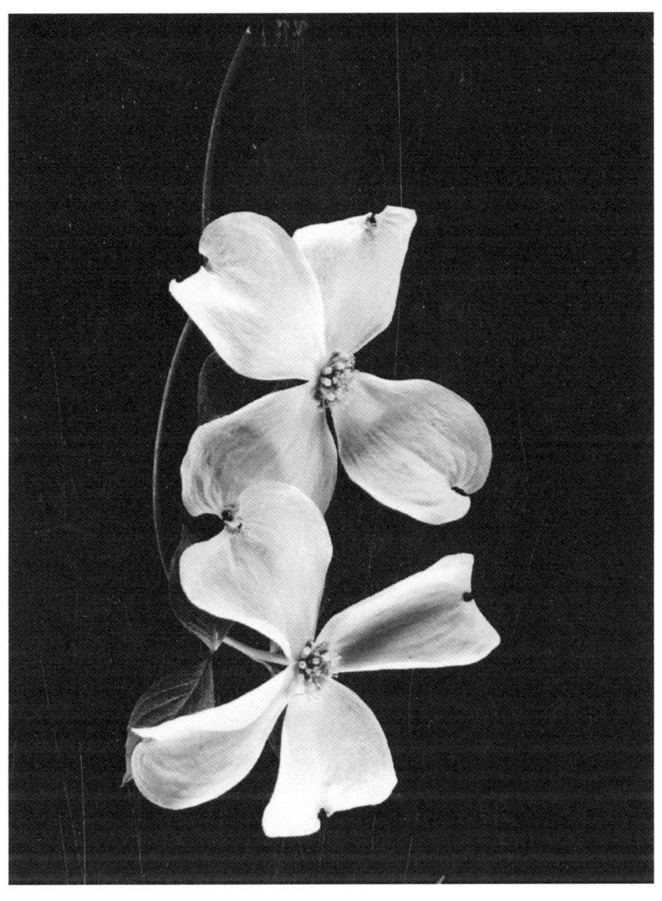

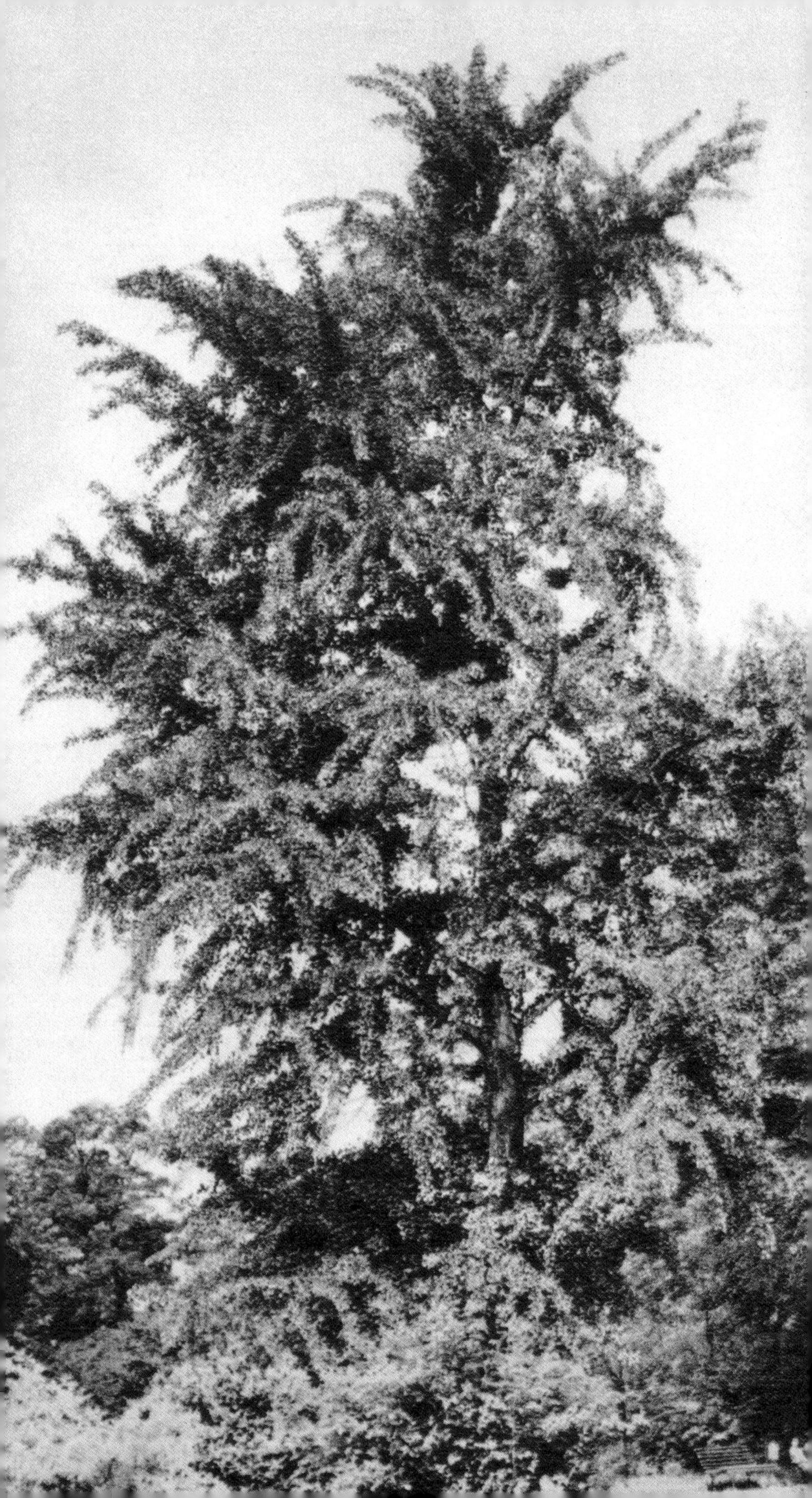

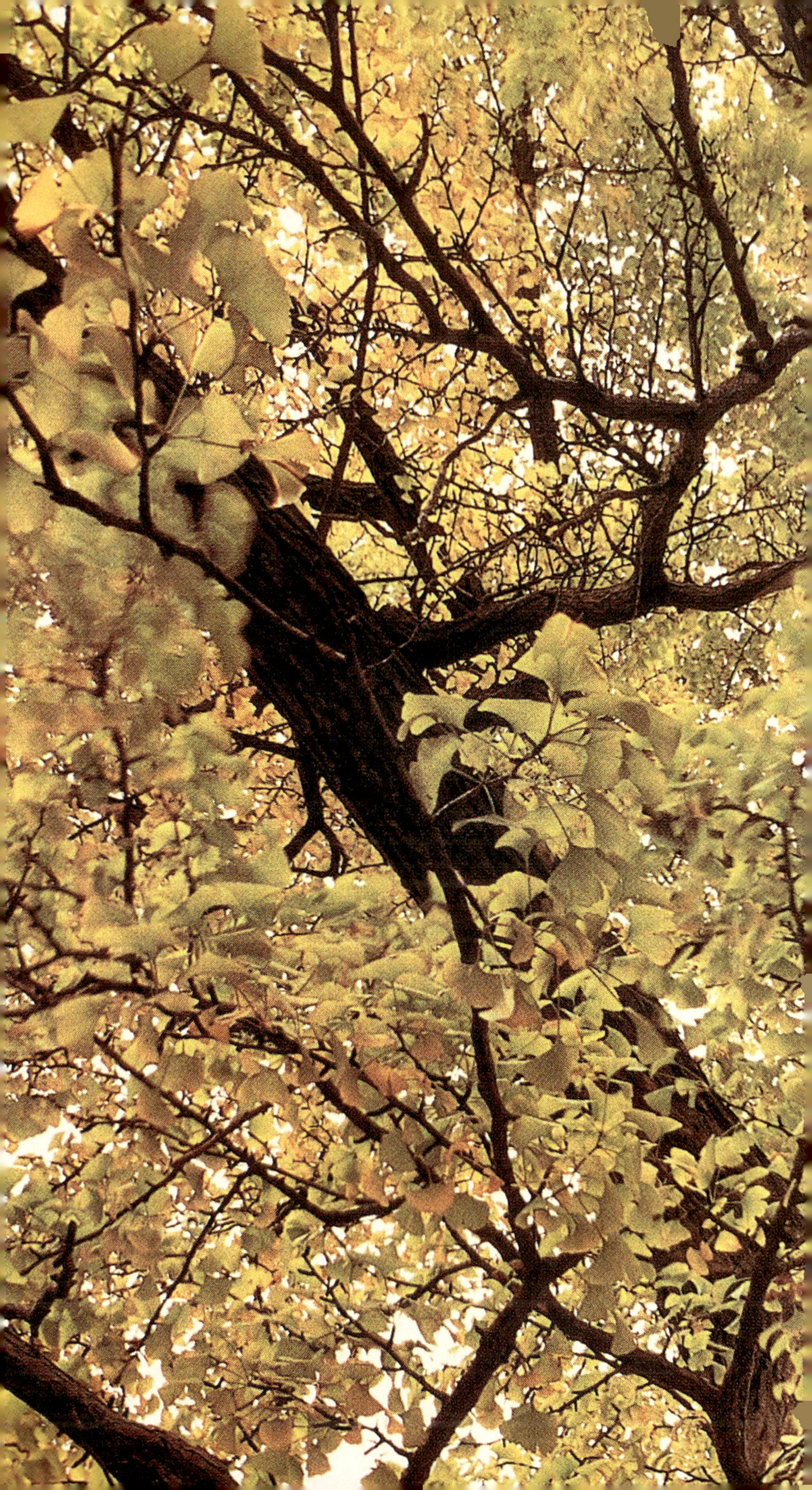

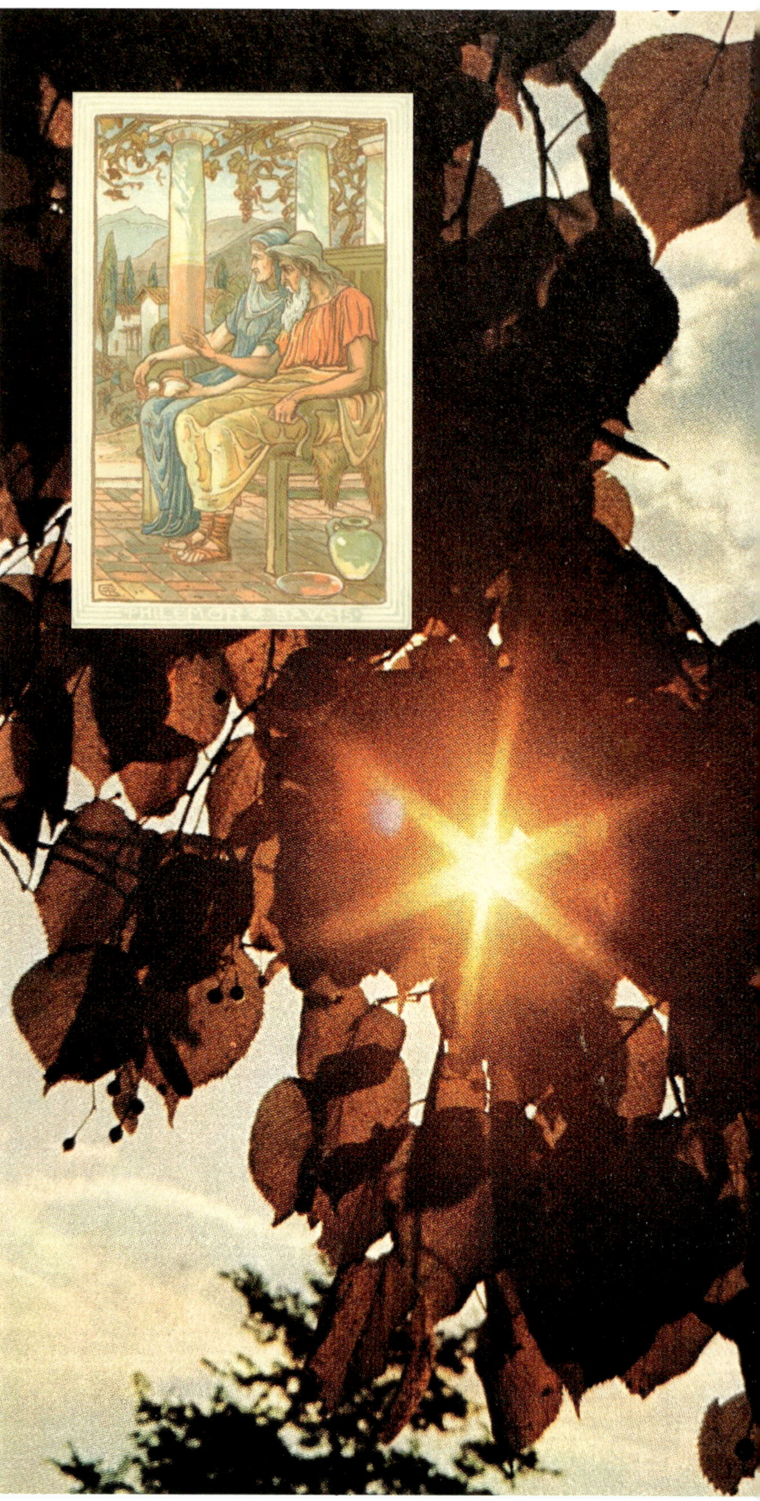

PHILEMON & BAVCIS

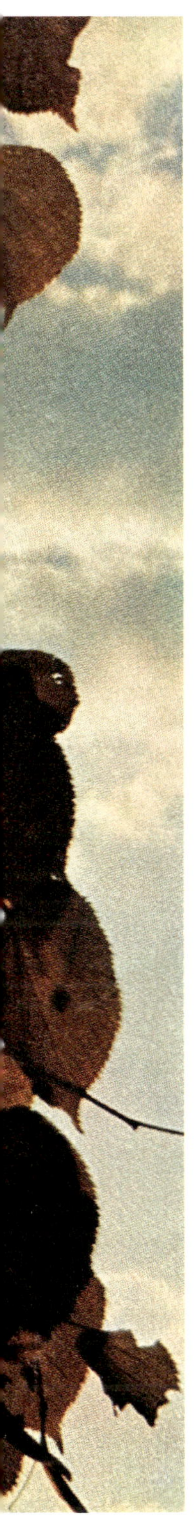

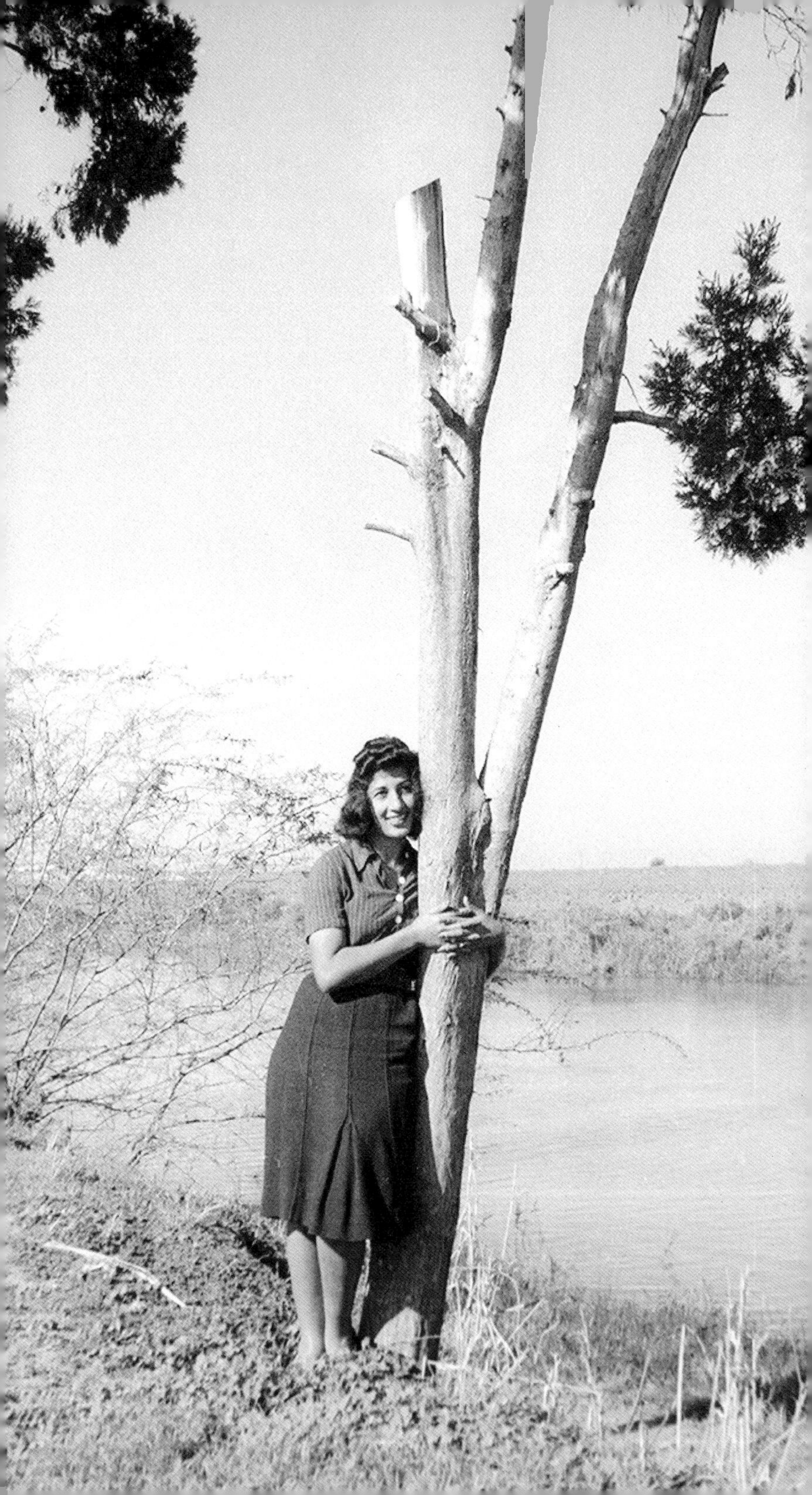

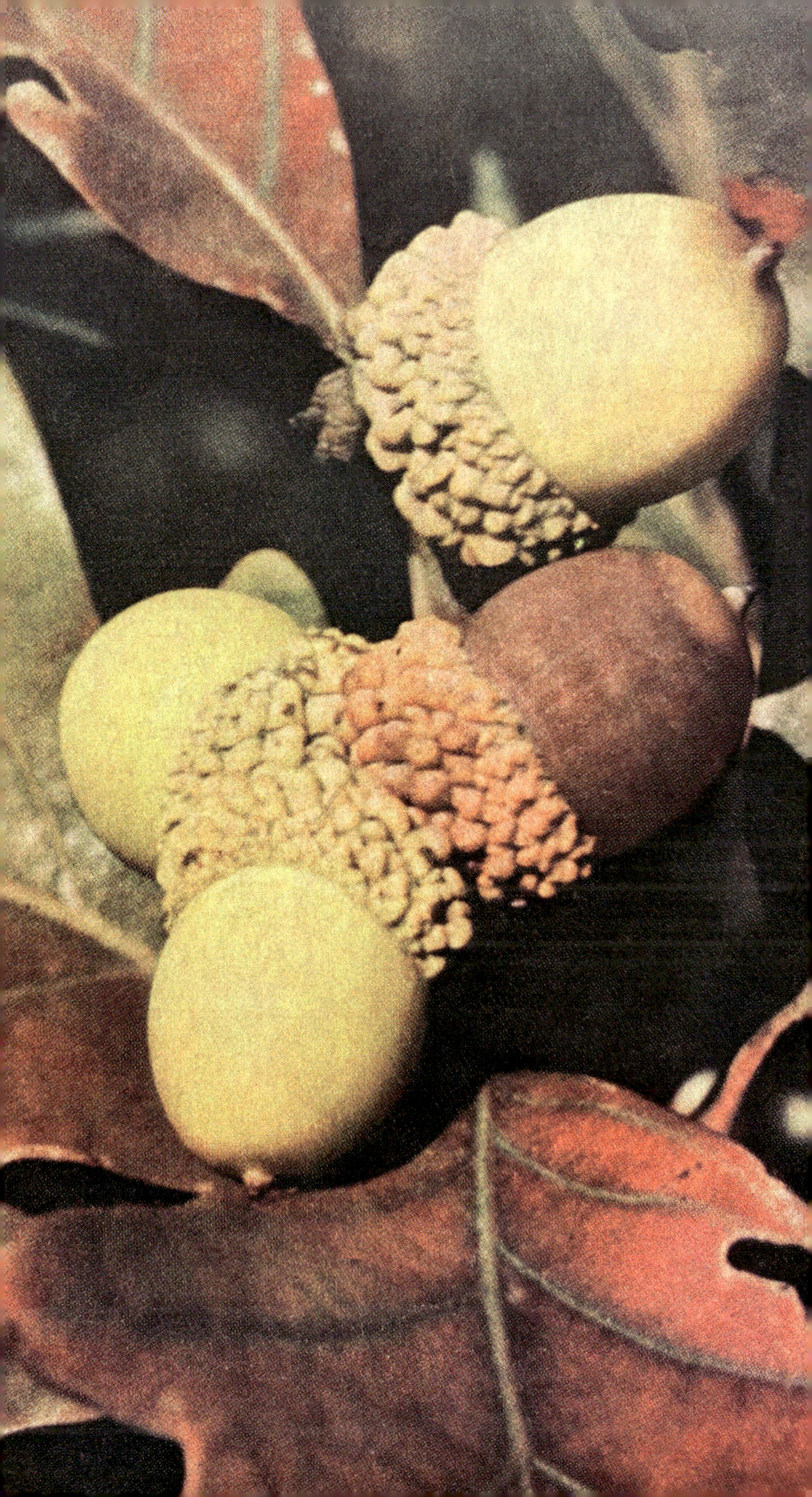

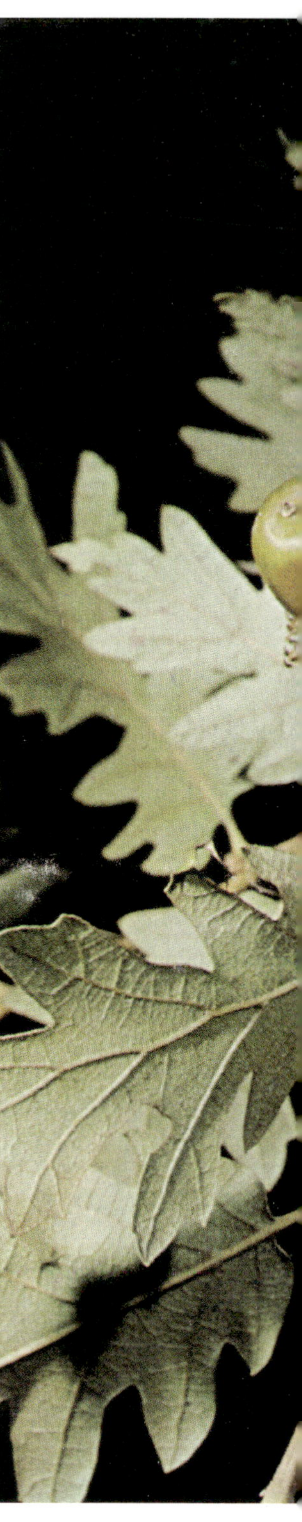

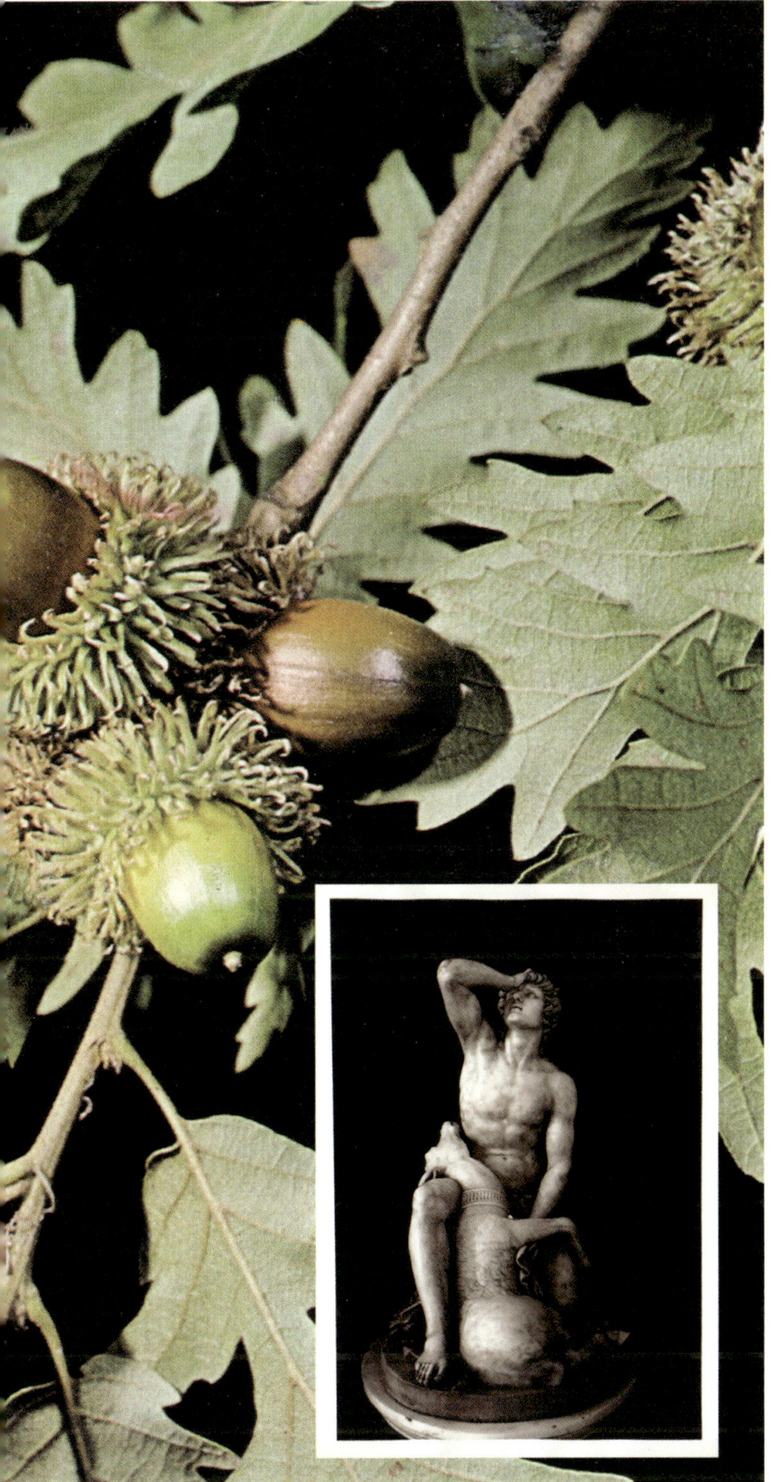

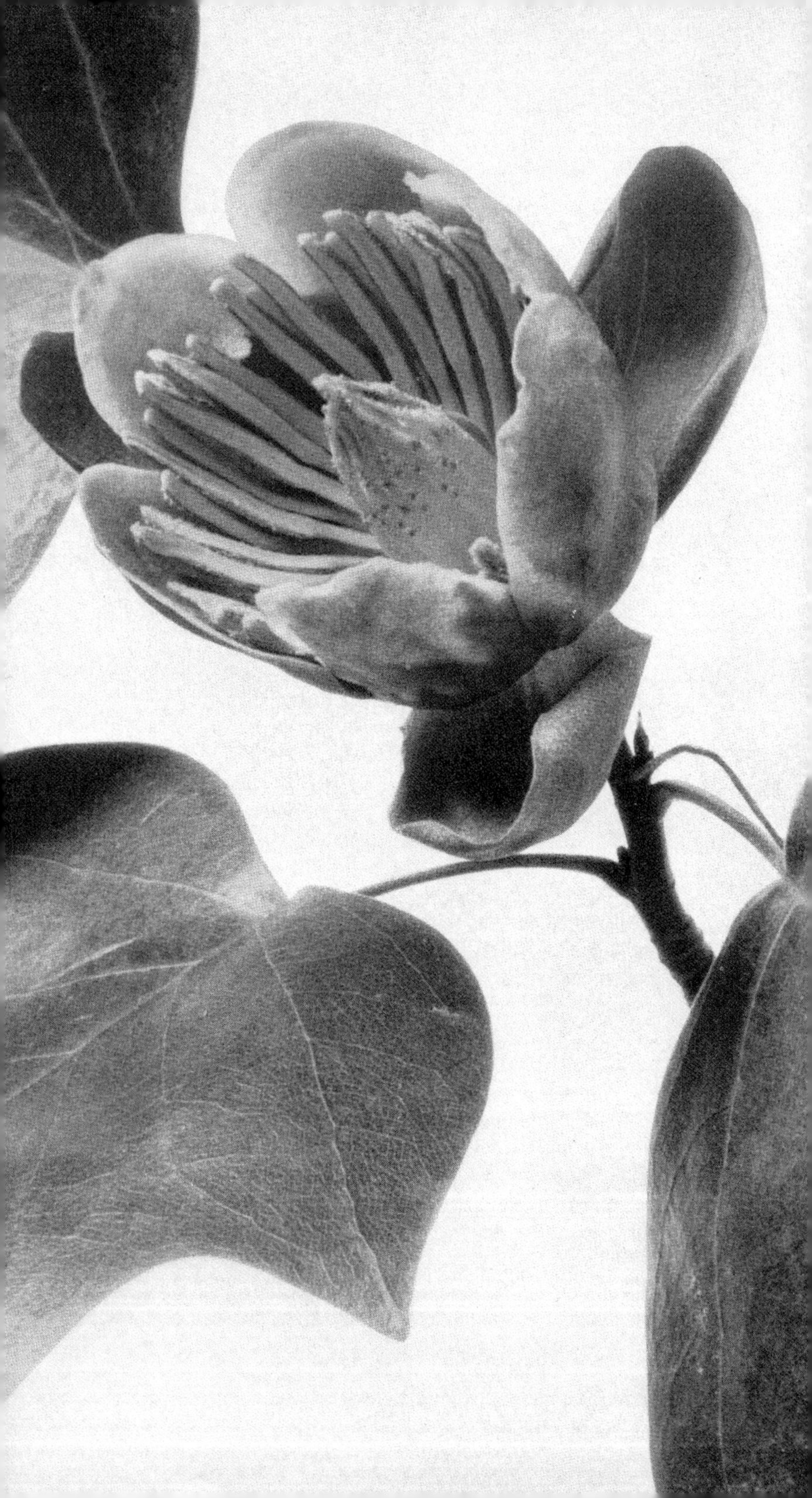

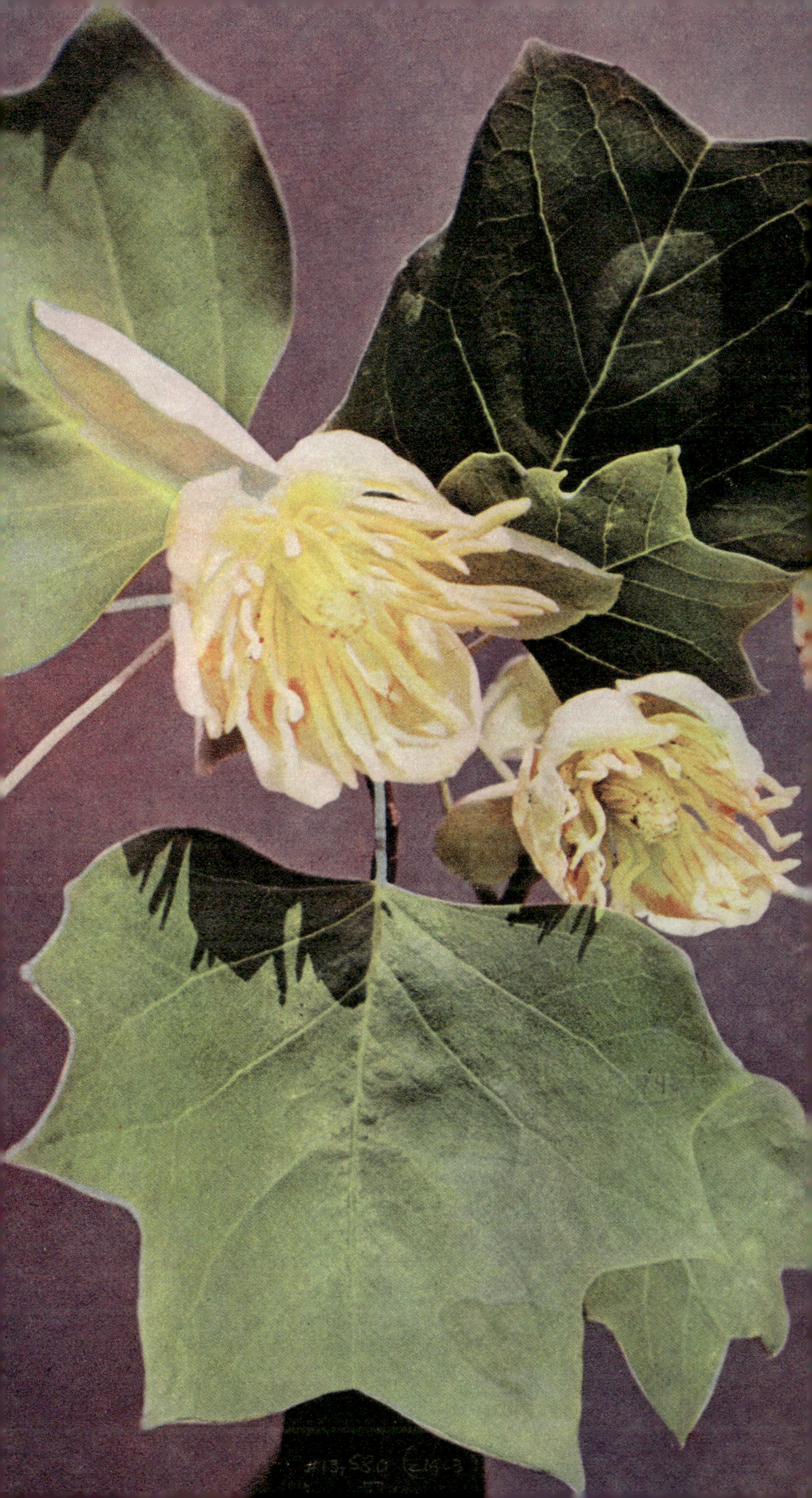

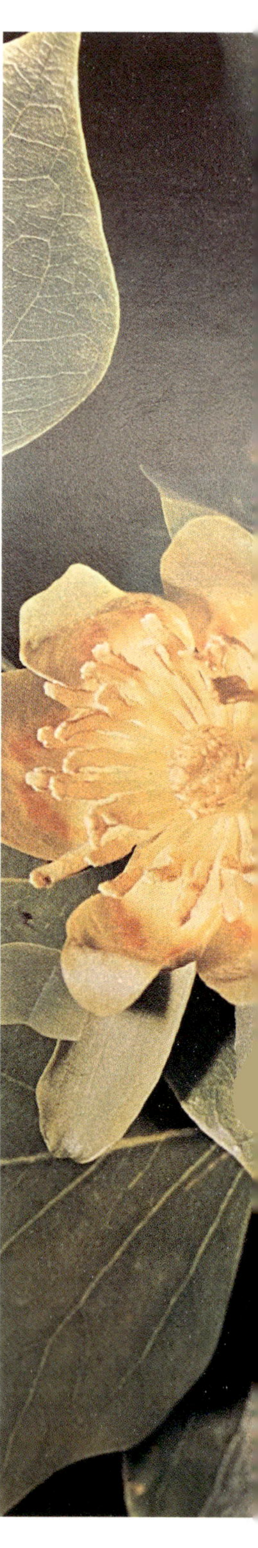

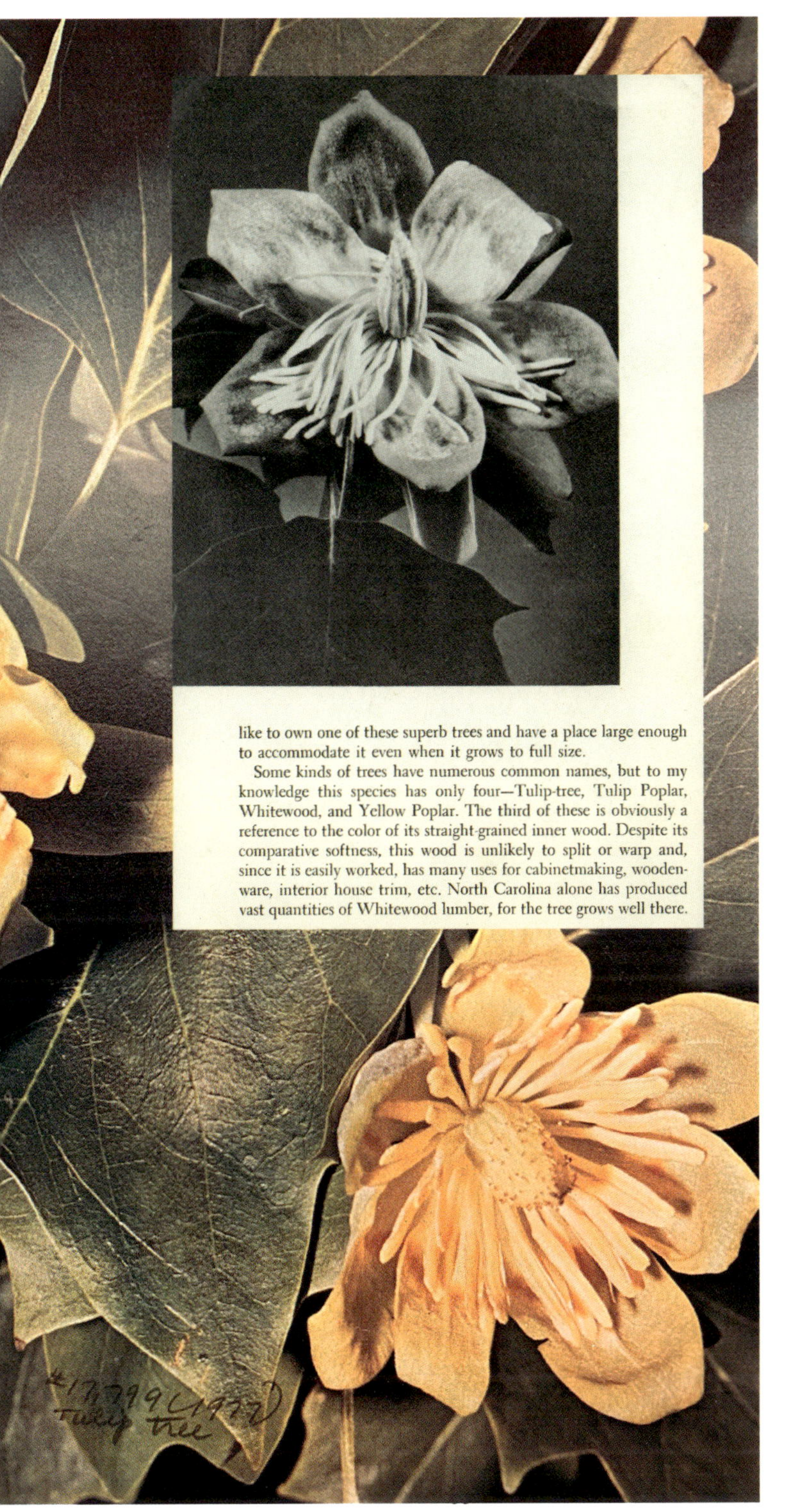

like to own one of these superb trees and have a place large enough to accommodate it even when it grows to full size.

Some kinds of trees have numerous common names, but to my knowledge this species has only four—Tulip-tree, Tulip Poplar, Whitewood, and Yellow Poplar. The third of these is obviously a reference to the color of its straight-grained inner wood. Despite its comparative softness, this wood is unlikely to split or warp and, since it is easily worked, has many uses for cabinetmaking, woodenware, interior house trim, etc. North Carolina alone has produced vast quantities of Whitewood lumber, for the tree grows well there.

near Dukes, Marquette County. Woolery standing by tree.
278164 - Old growth white pine in mixed hardwood stand,
Dukes, Michigan. 5/20/33

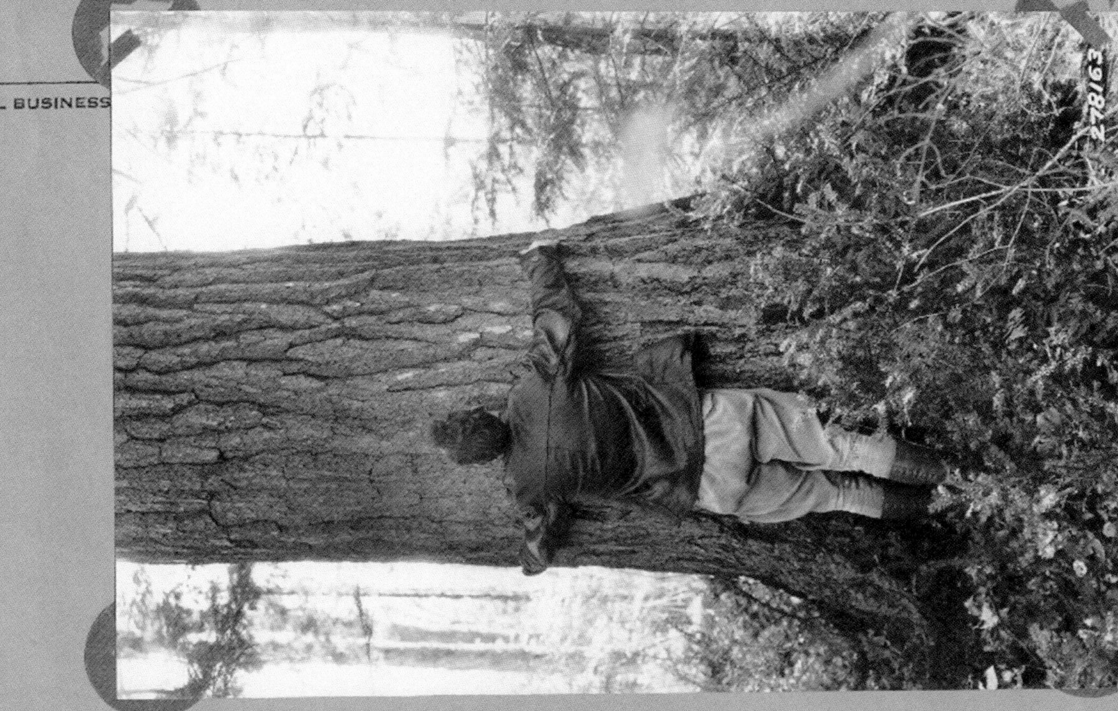

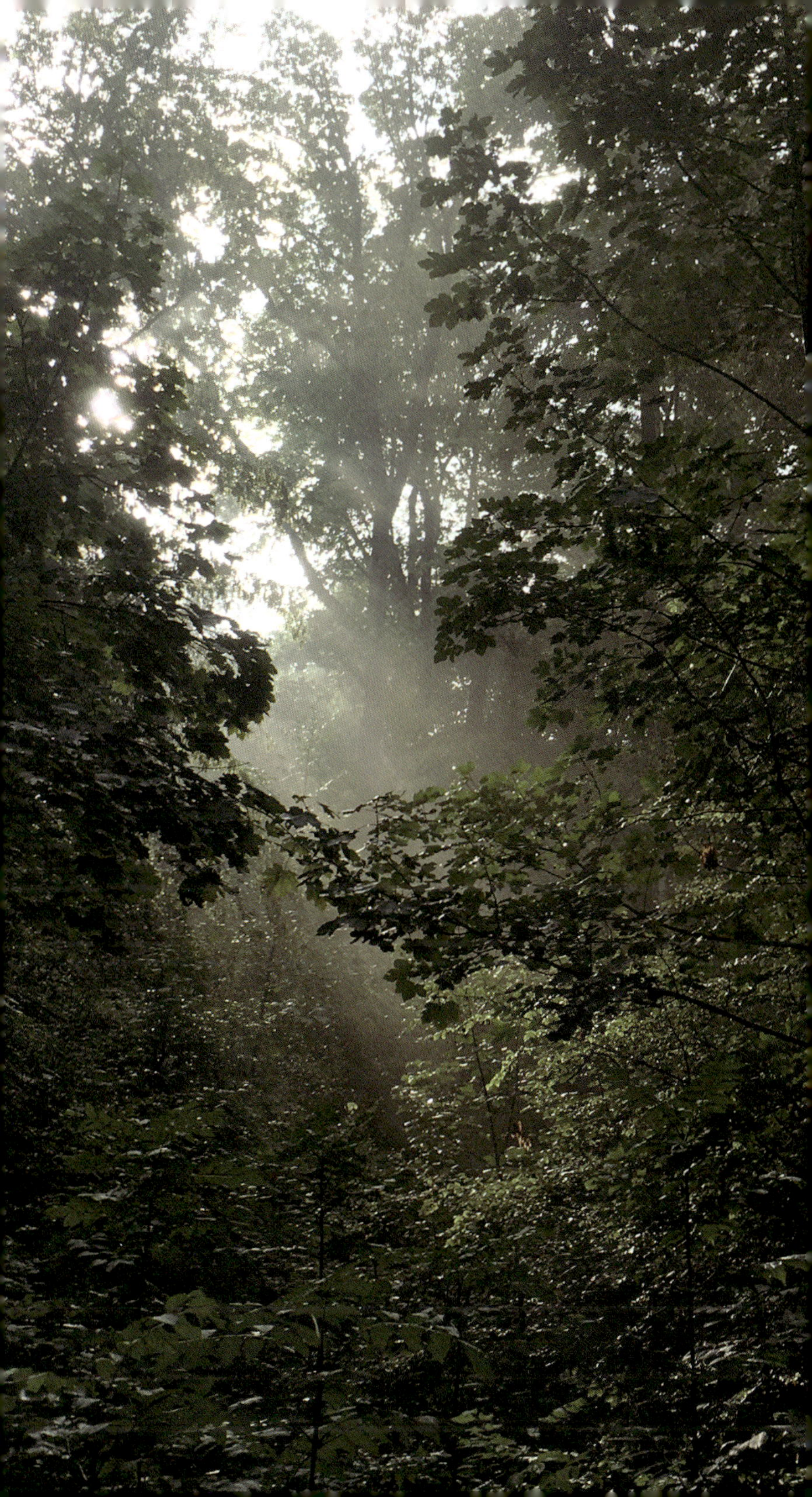

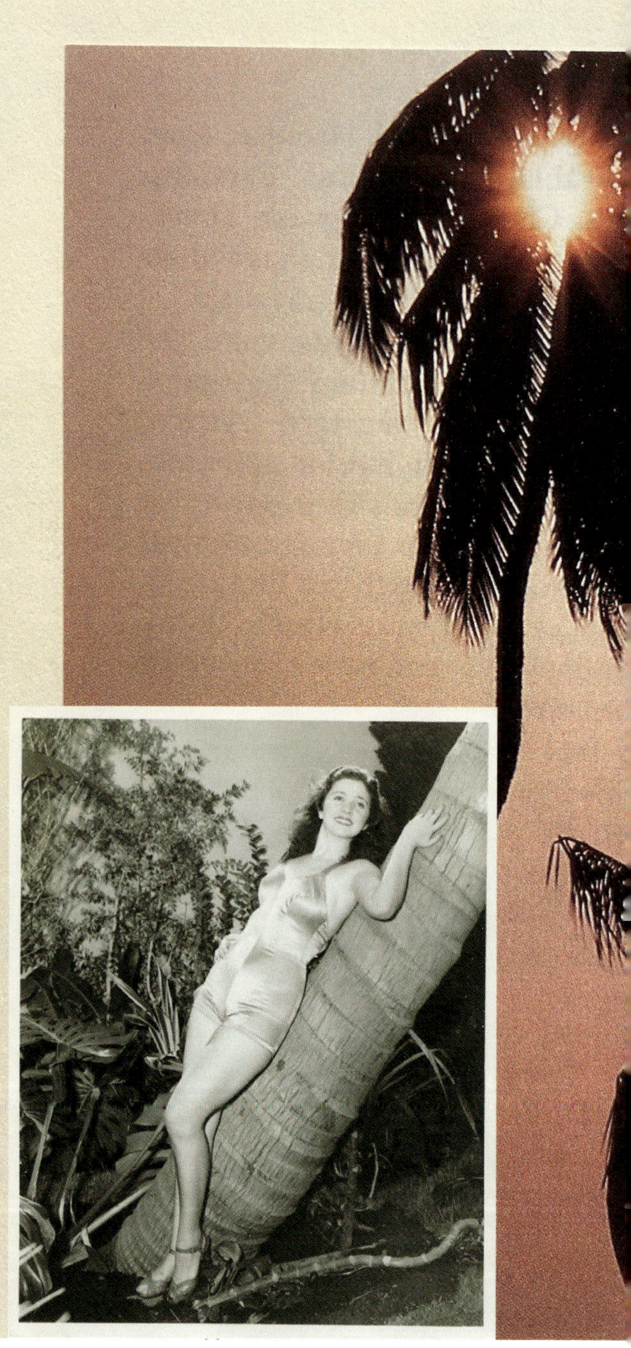

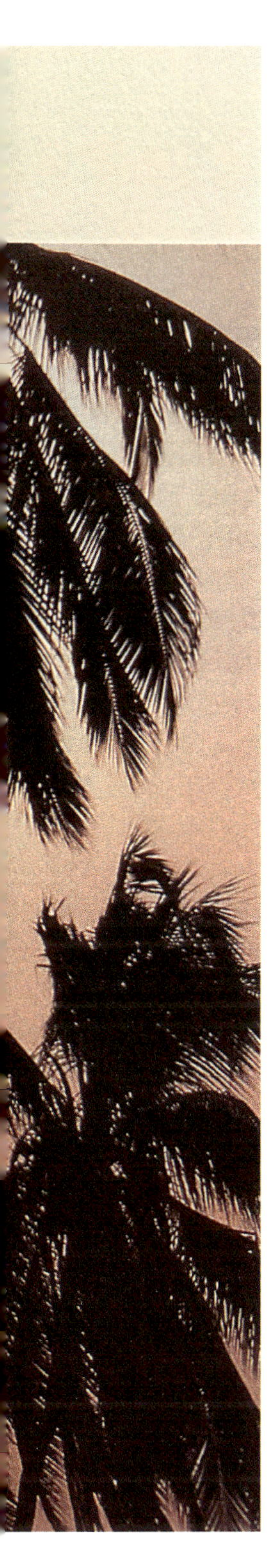

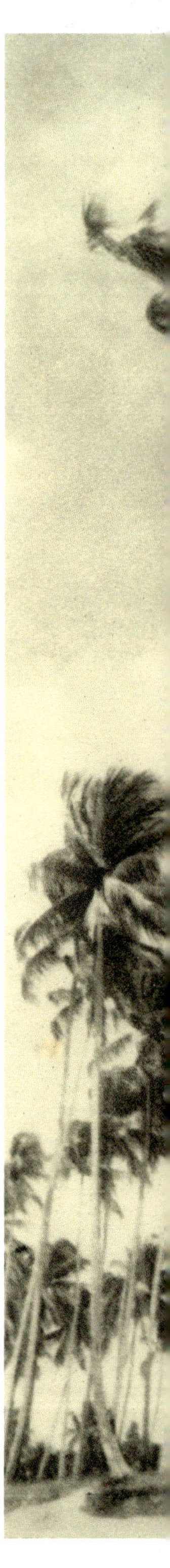

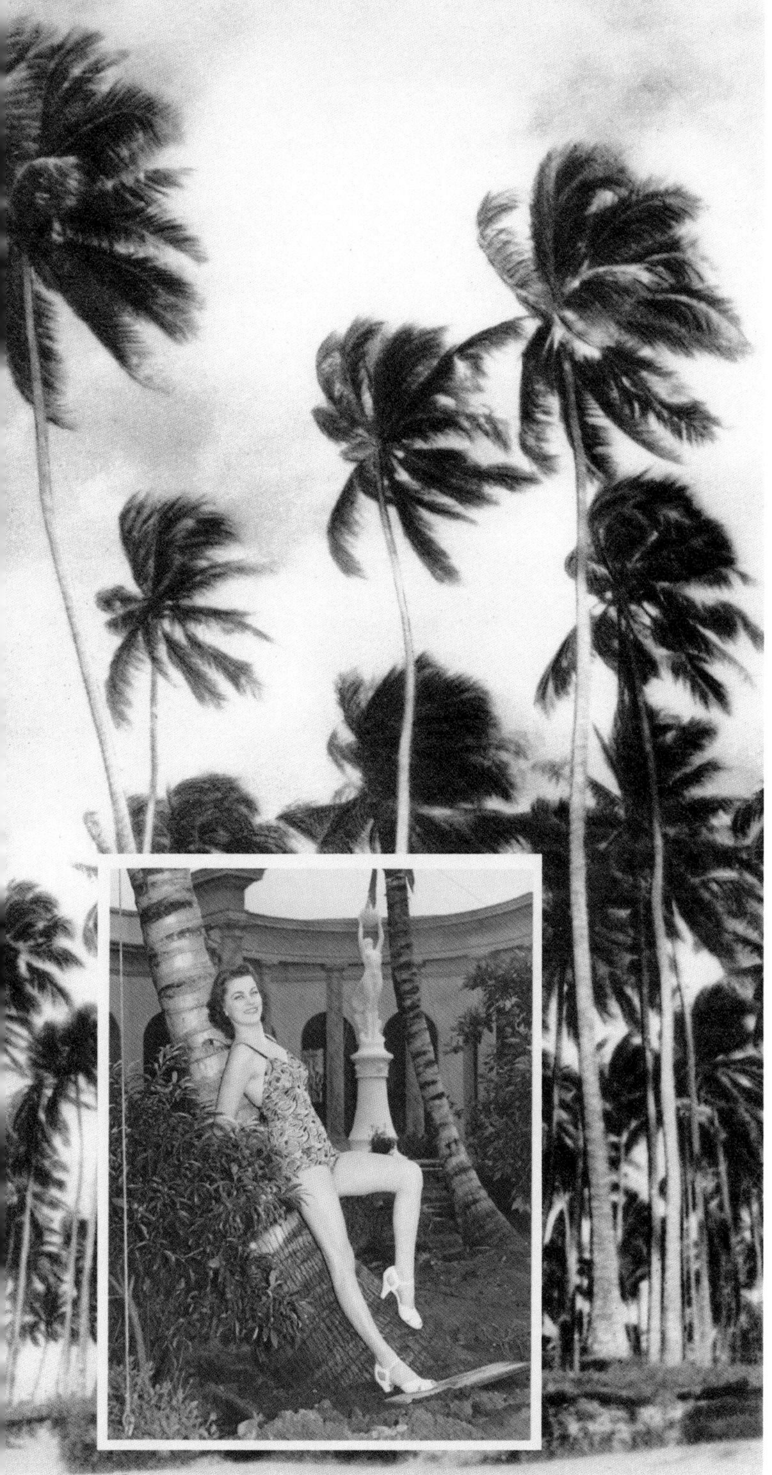

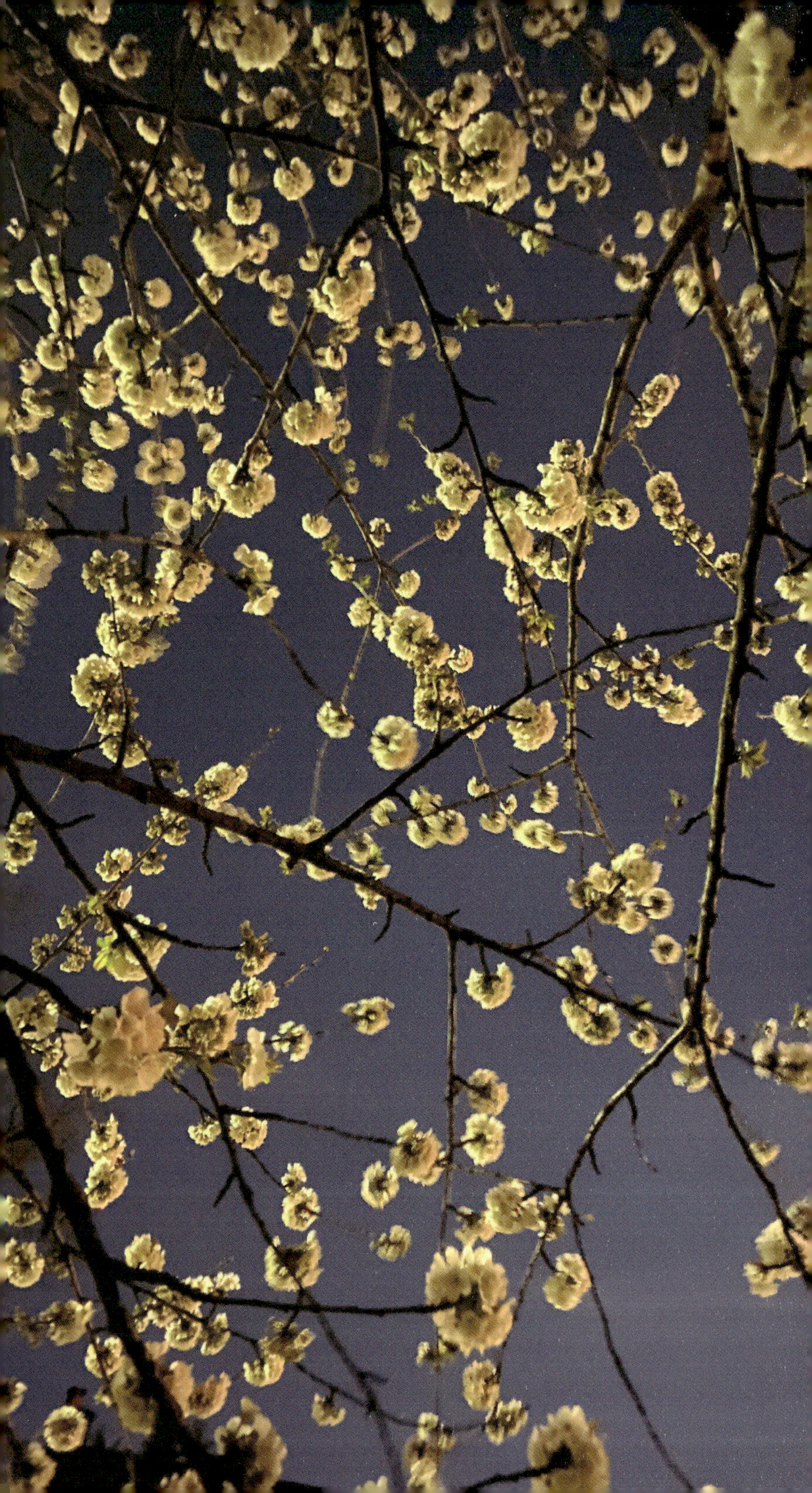

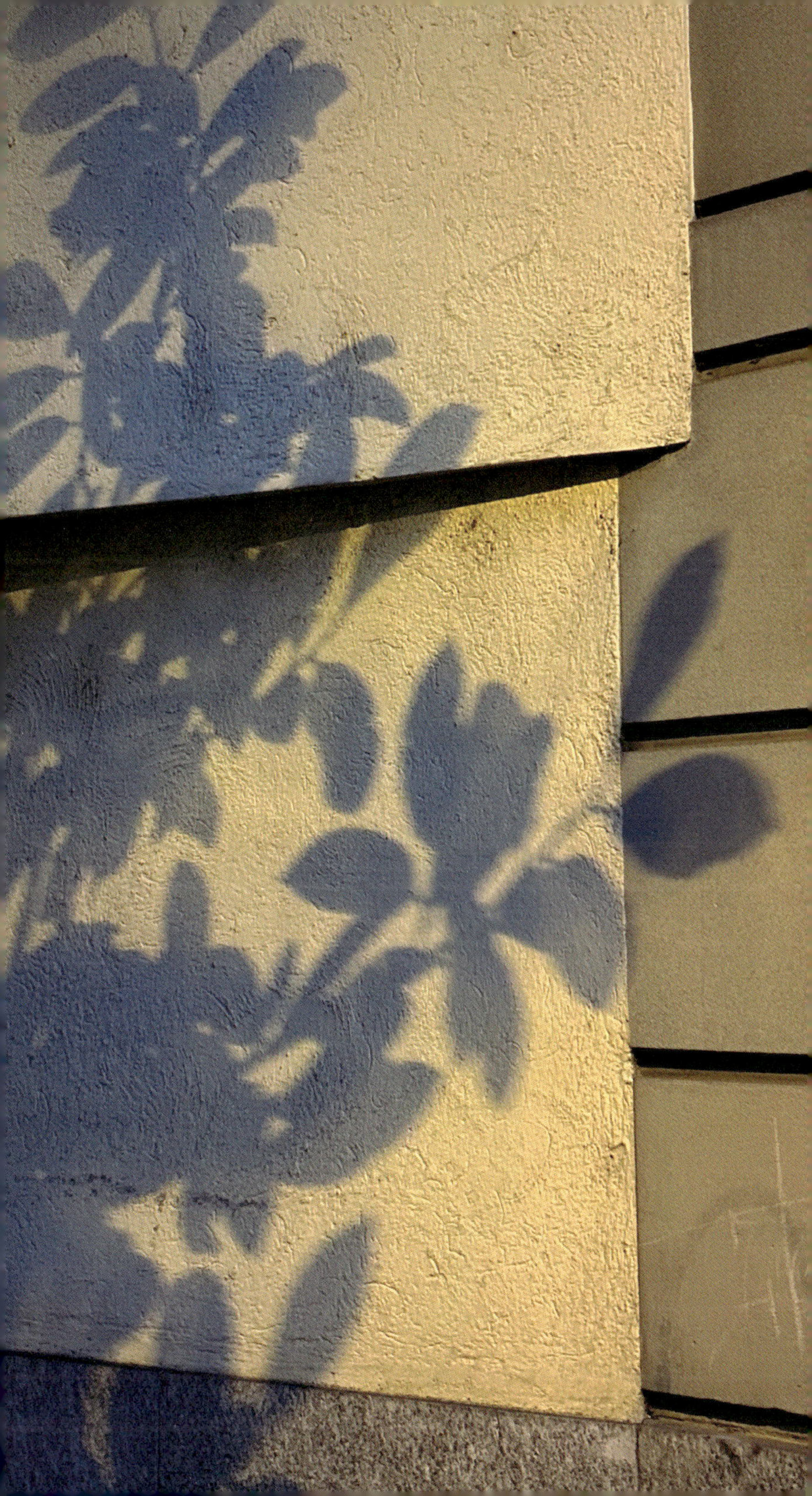

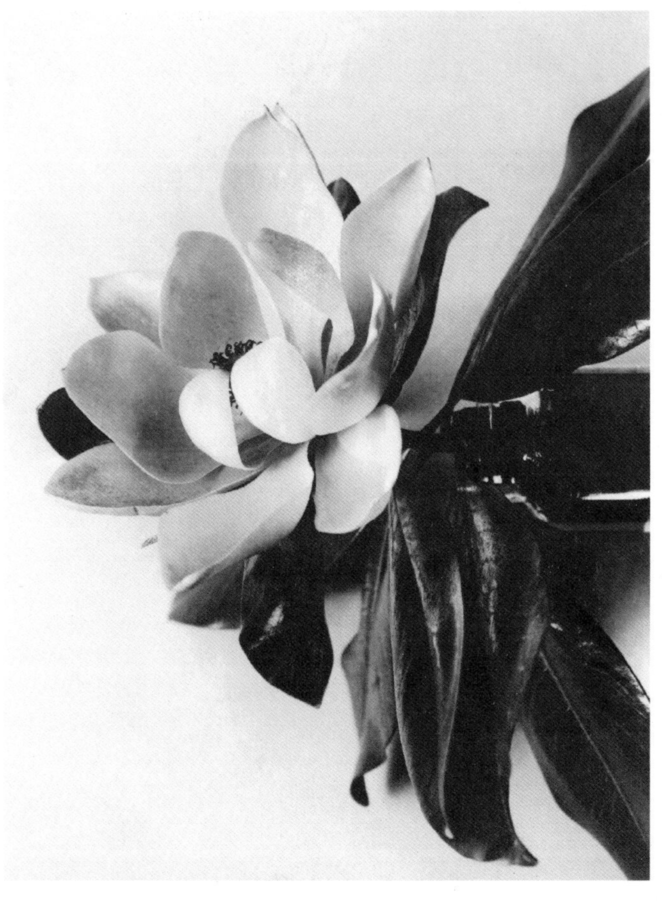

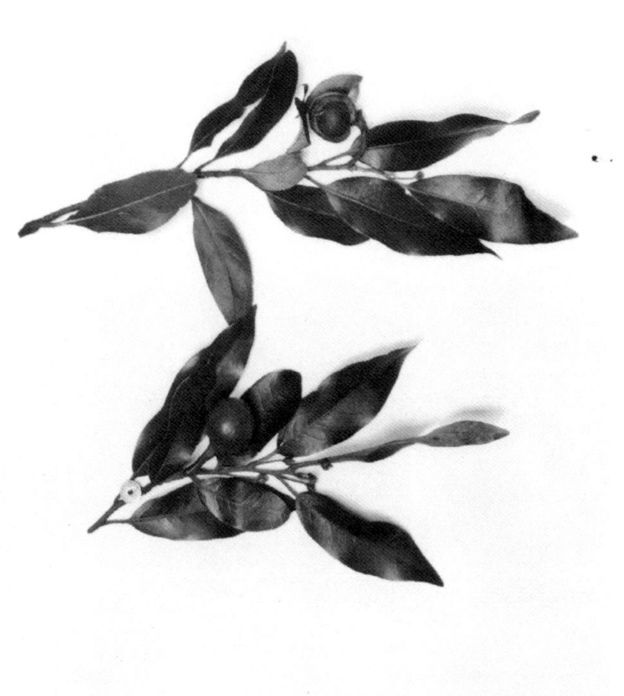

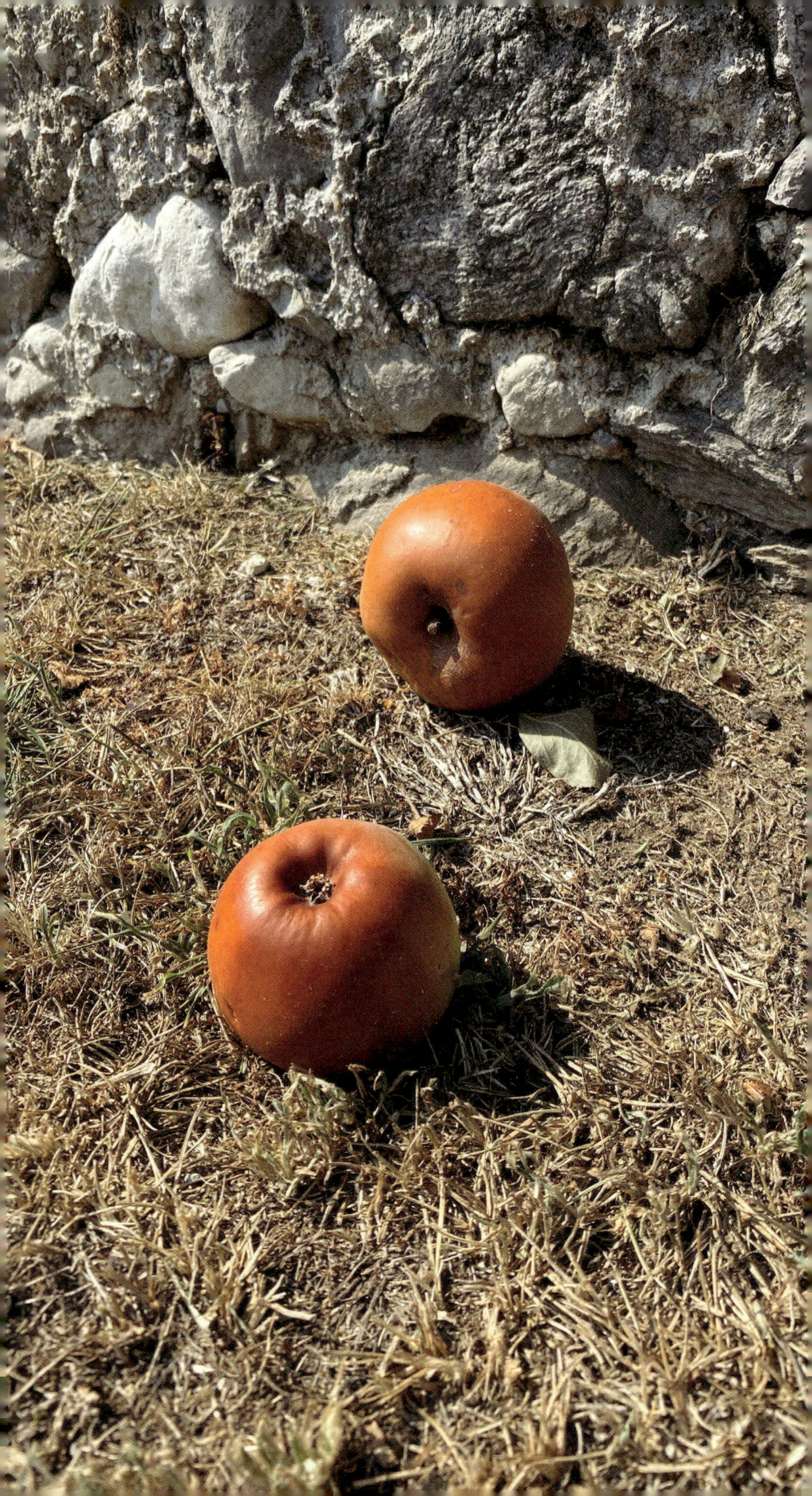

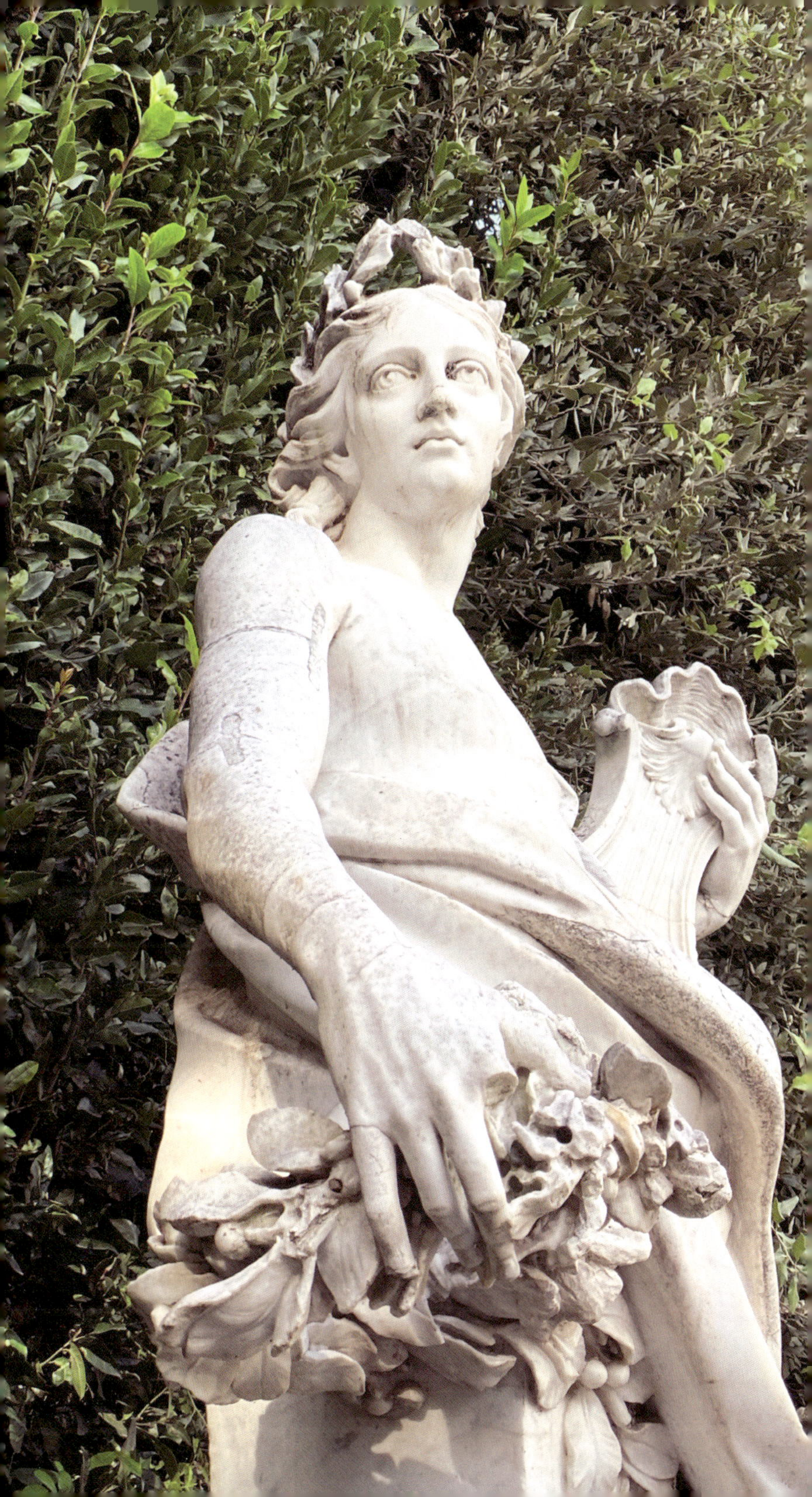

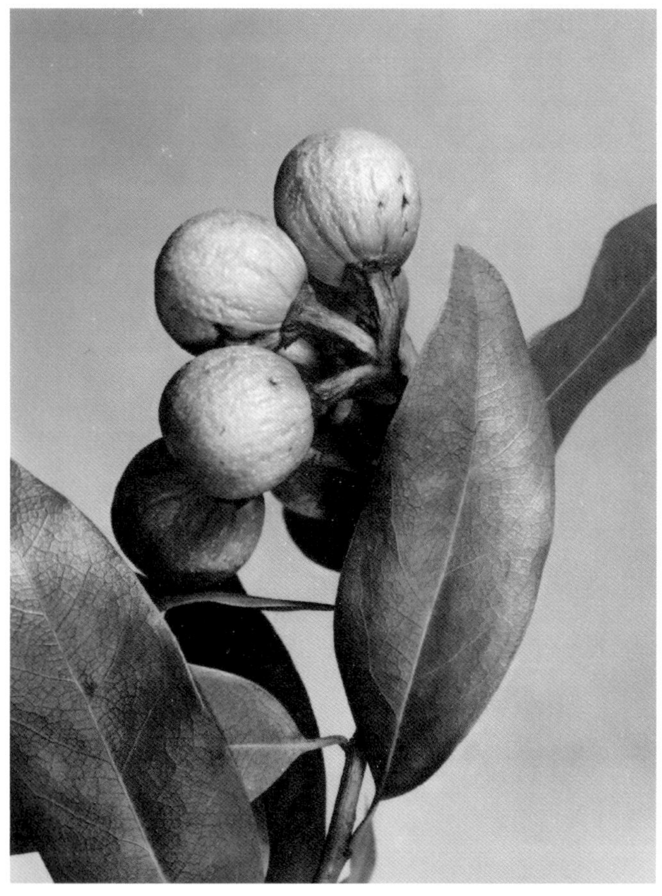

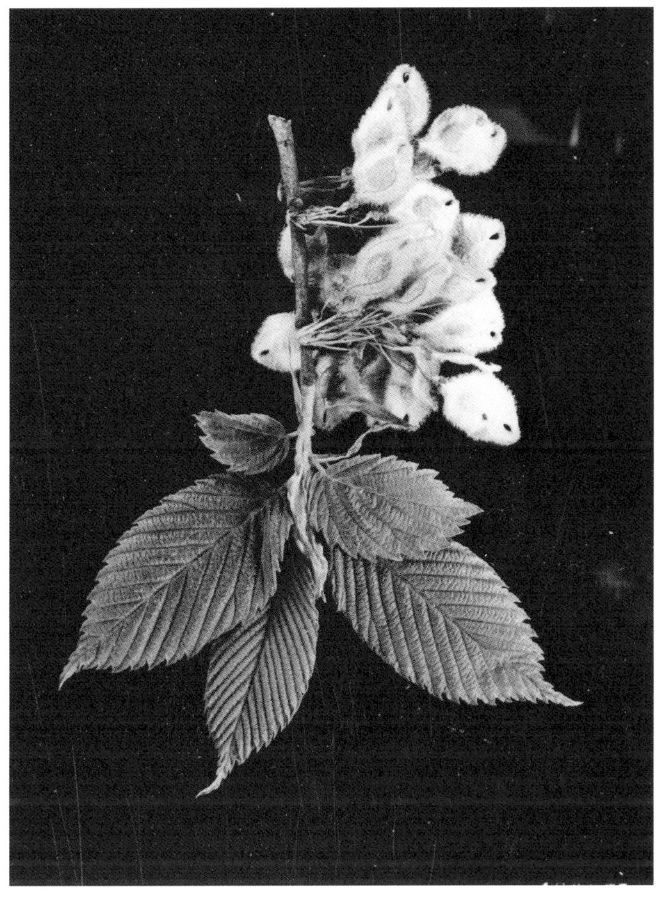

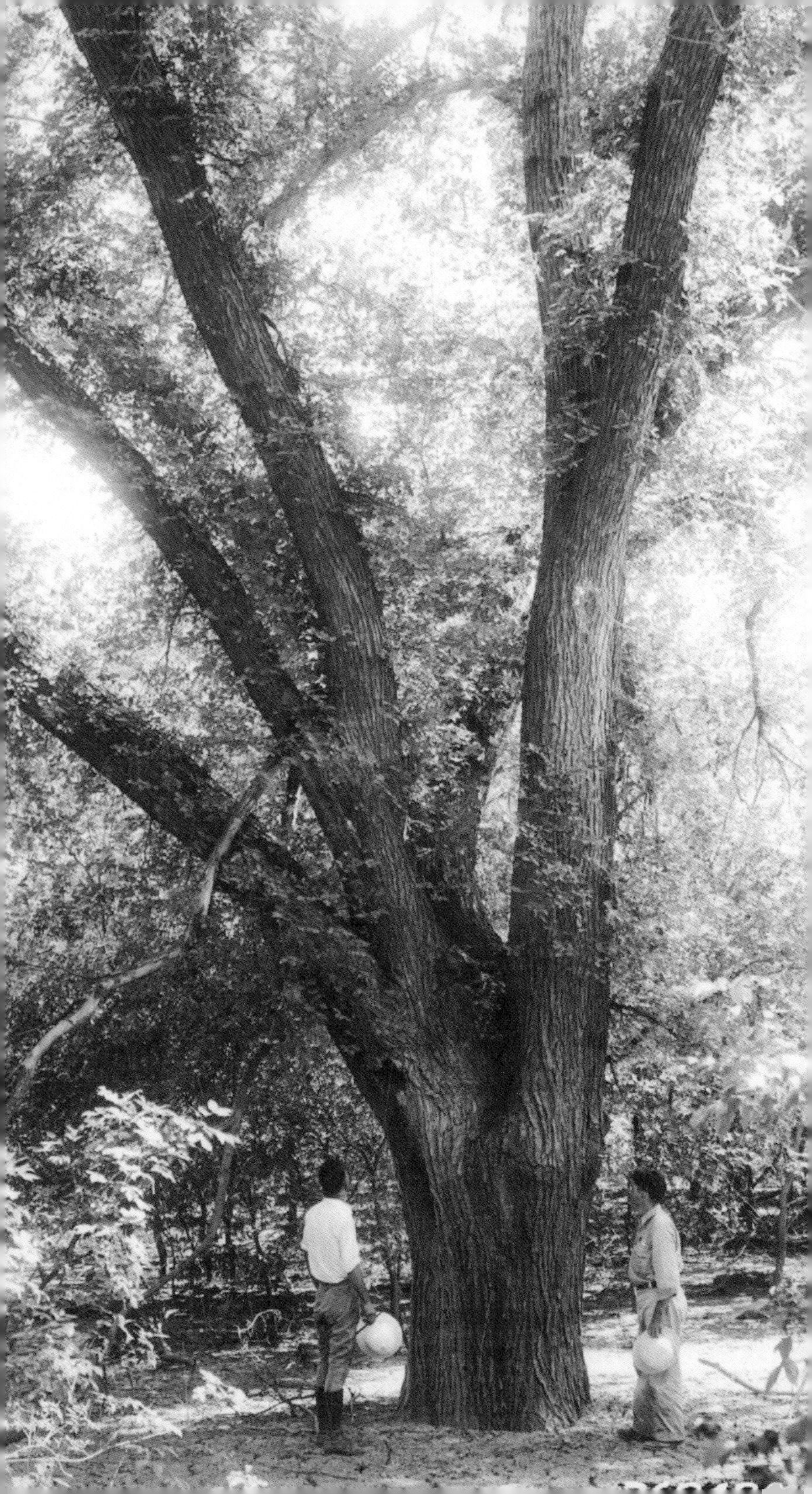

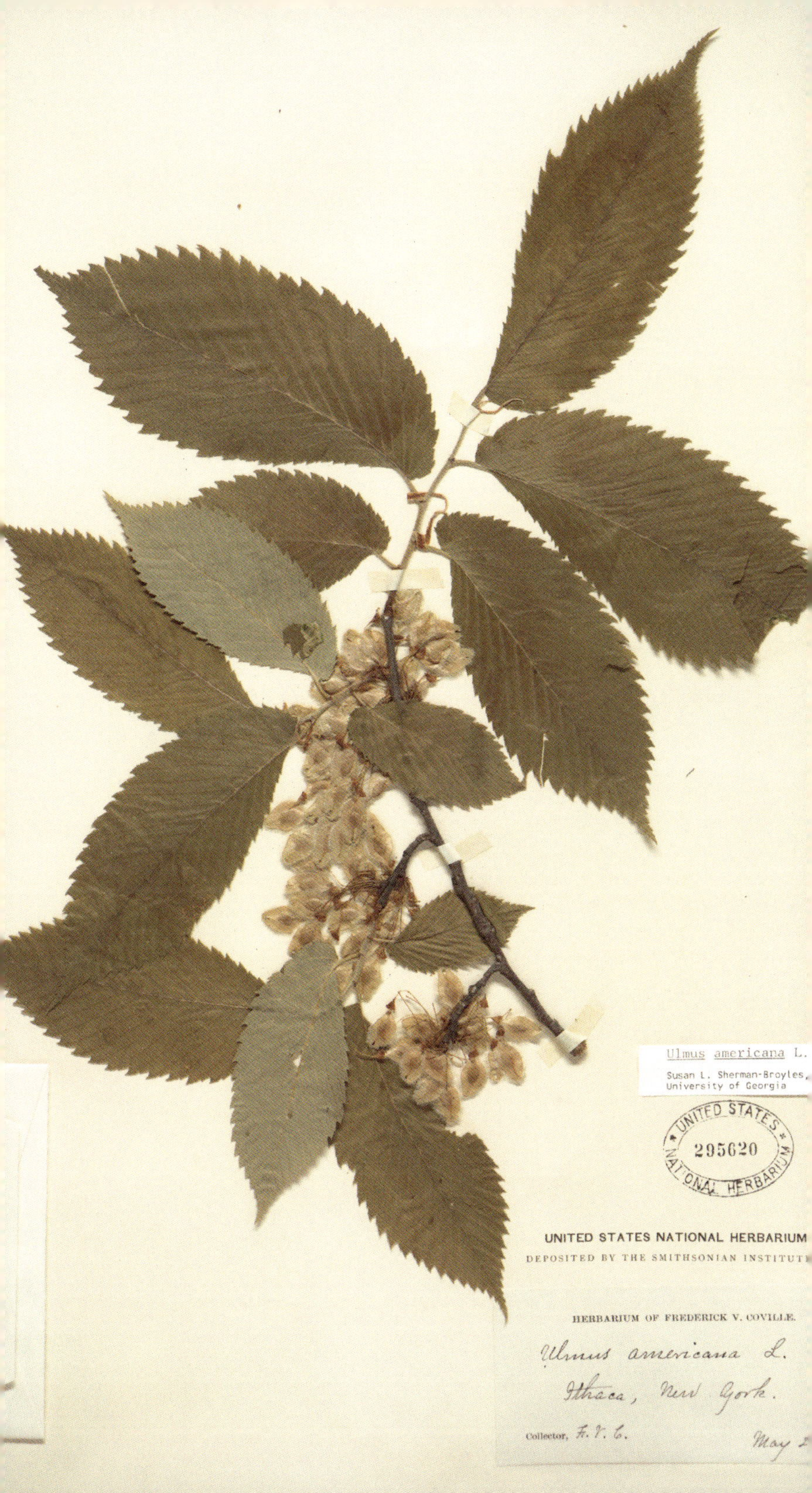
Ulmus americana L.
Susan L. Sherman-Broyles,
University of Georgia
UNITED STATES
295620
NATIONAL HERBARIUM
UNITED STATES NATIONAL HERBARIUM
DEPOSITED BY THE SMITHSONIAN INSTITUTE
HERBARIUM OF FREDERICK V. COVILLE.
Ulmus americana L.
Ithaca, New York.
Collector, F. V. C.          May

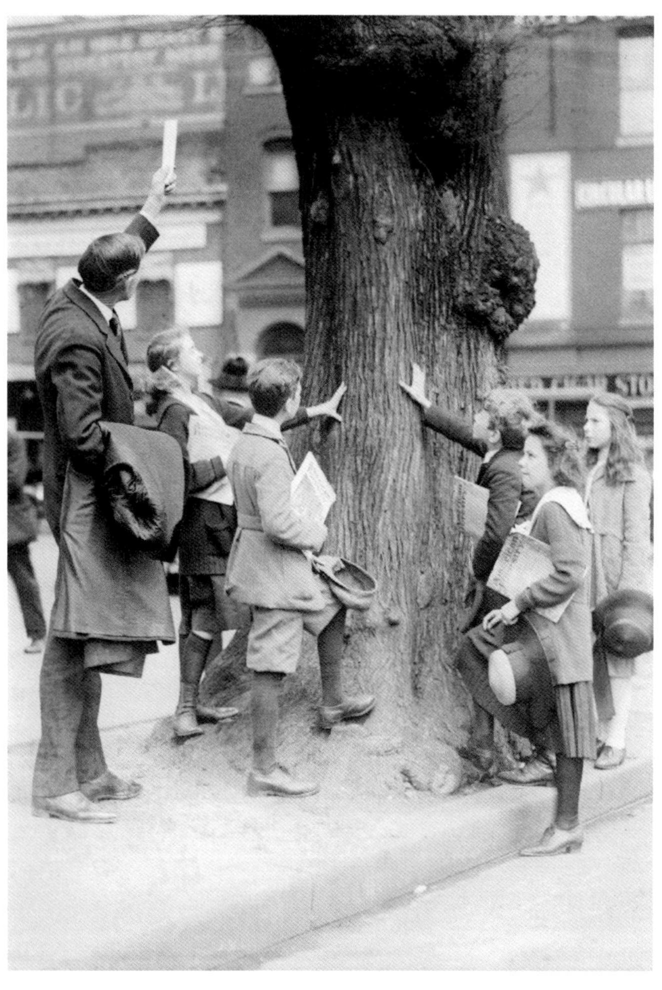

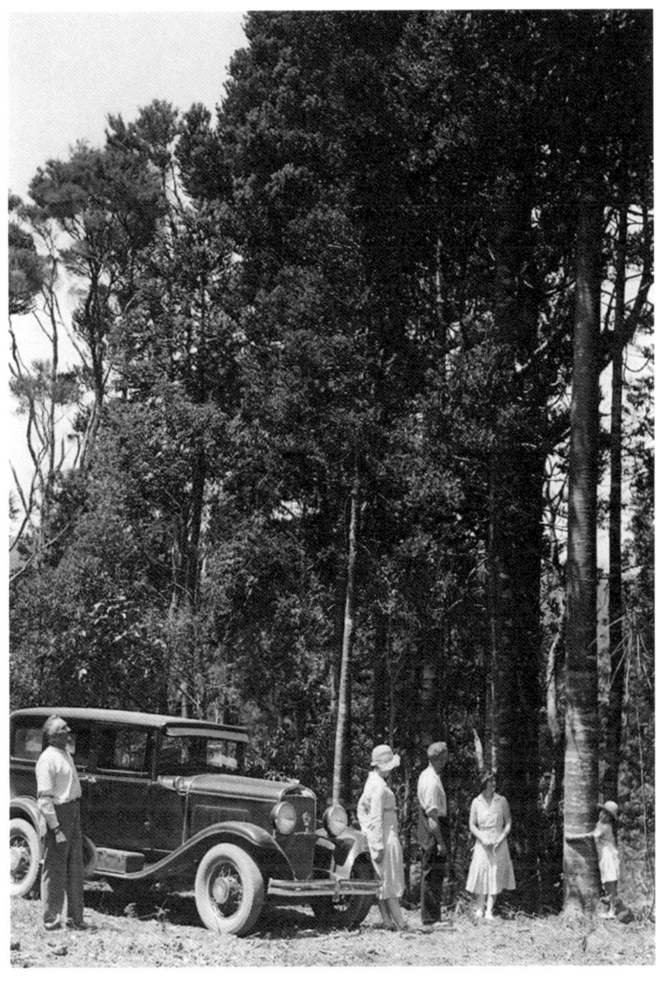

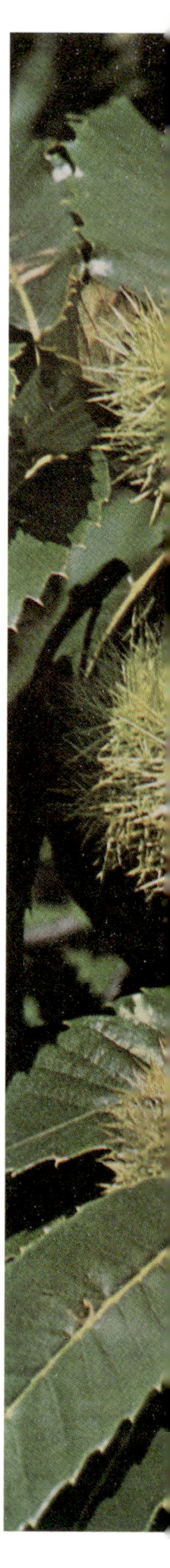

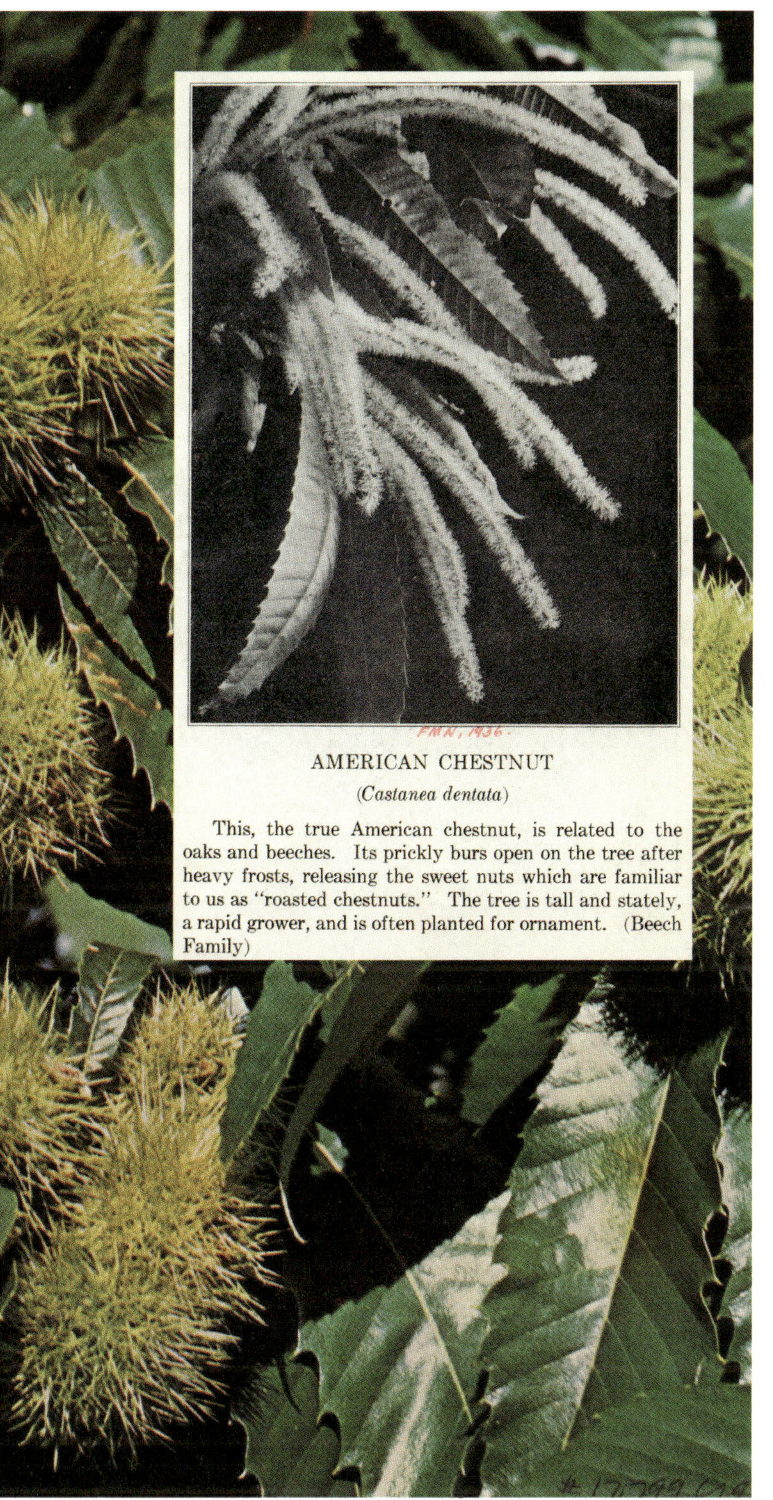


## AMERICAN CHESTNUT

### (*Castanea dentata*)

This, the true American chestnut, is related to the oaks and beeches. Its prickly burs open on the tree after heavy frosts, releasing the sweet nuts which are familiar to us as "roasted chestnuts." The tree is tall and stately, a rapid grower, and is often planted for ornament. (Beech Family)

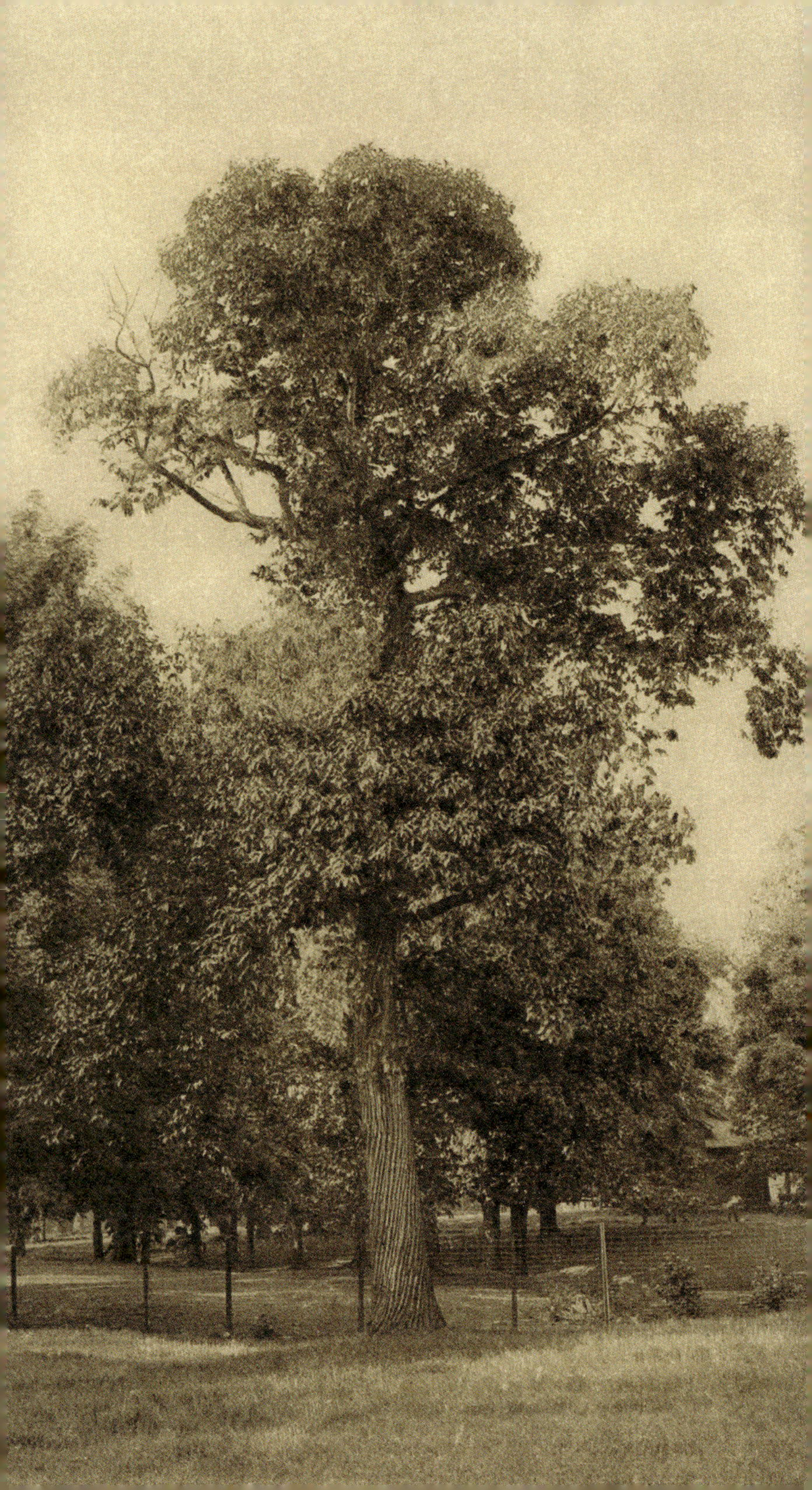

October 19, 1959


United States Department of Agriculture
Forest Service
Albert G. Snow, Jr.
Research Center Leader
RFD 2 Box 263
Laurel, Maryland

Attention: Mr. J. D. Diller

Dear Sir:

    Thank you for your letter of 3 September, 1959.

    I am sending herewith leaves and burrs from the 8" chestnut.  Please tell me if it is surely American.  Just lately this tree shows some blight on trunk.  Can small individual spots such as this be treated to kill it?

    I will be very happy to send scions in February.  -  Just give me instructions.


    Each of two other young trees- 2" show blight where wounded by falling branches.

                Very truly yours,

                Herbert F. Darling.

Encl.
HFD/lh

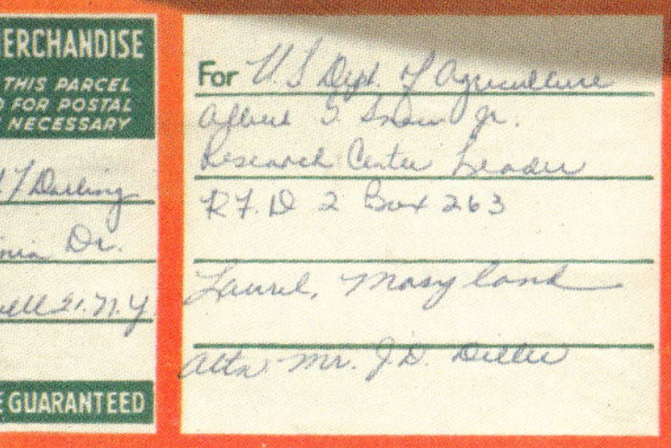

Image No.
03400304

PLANTS OF NEW YORK

Castanea dentata (Marsh.) Borkh.


Williamsville, New York.


Herbert F. Darling        Octobe
& J. D. Diller

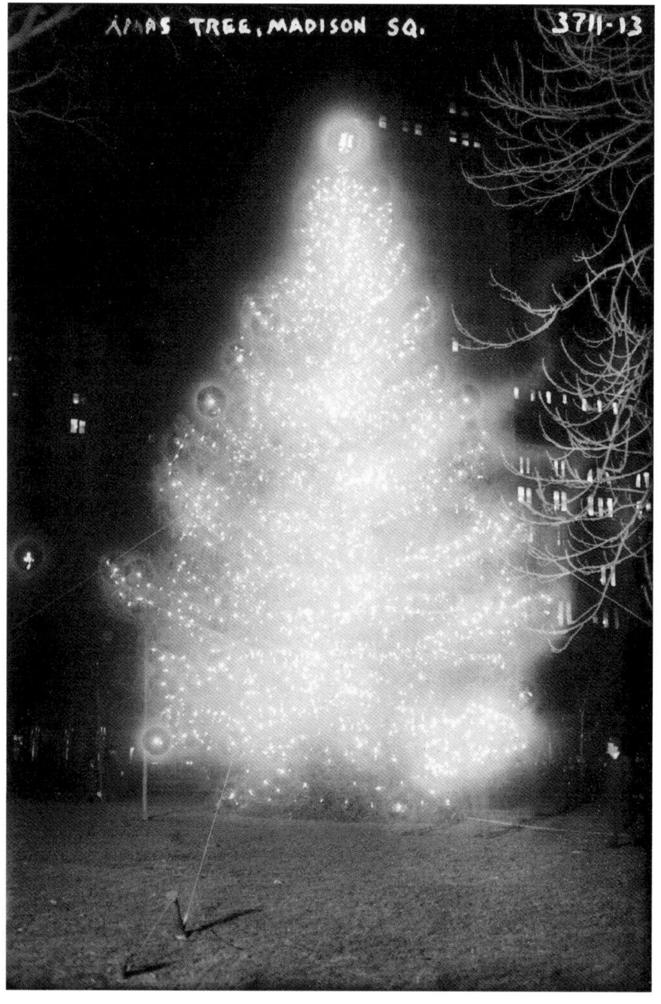
XMAS TREE, MADISON SQ.
3711-13

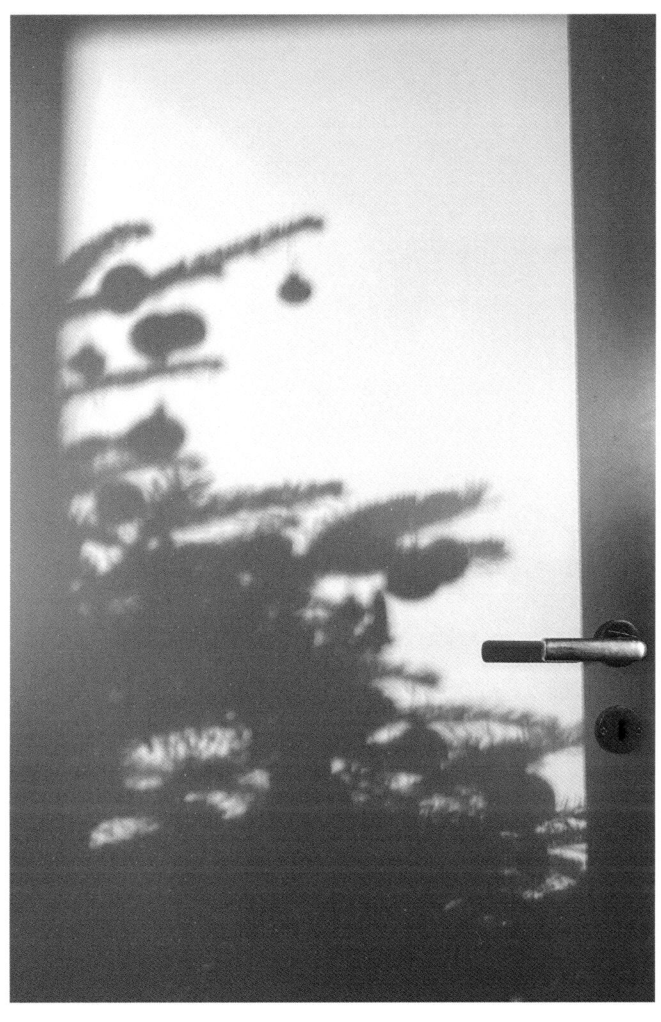

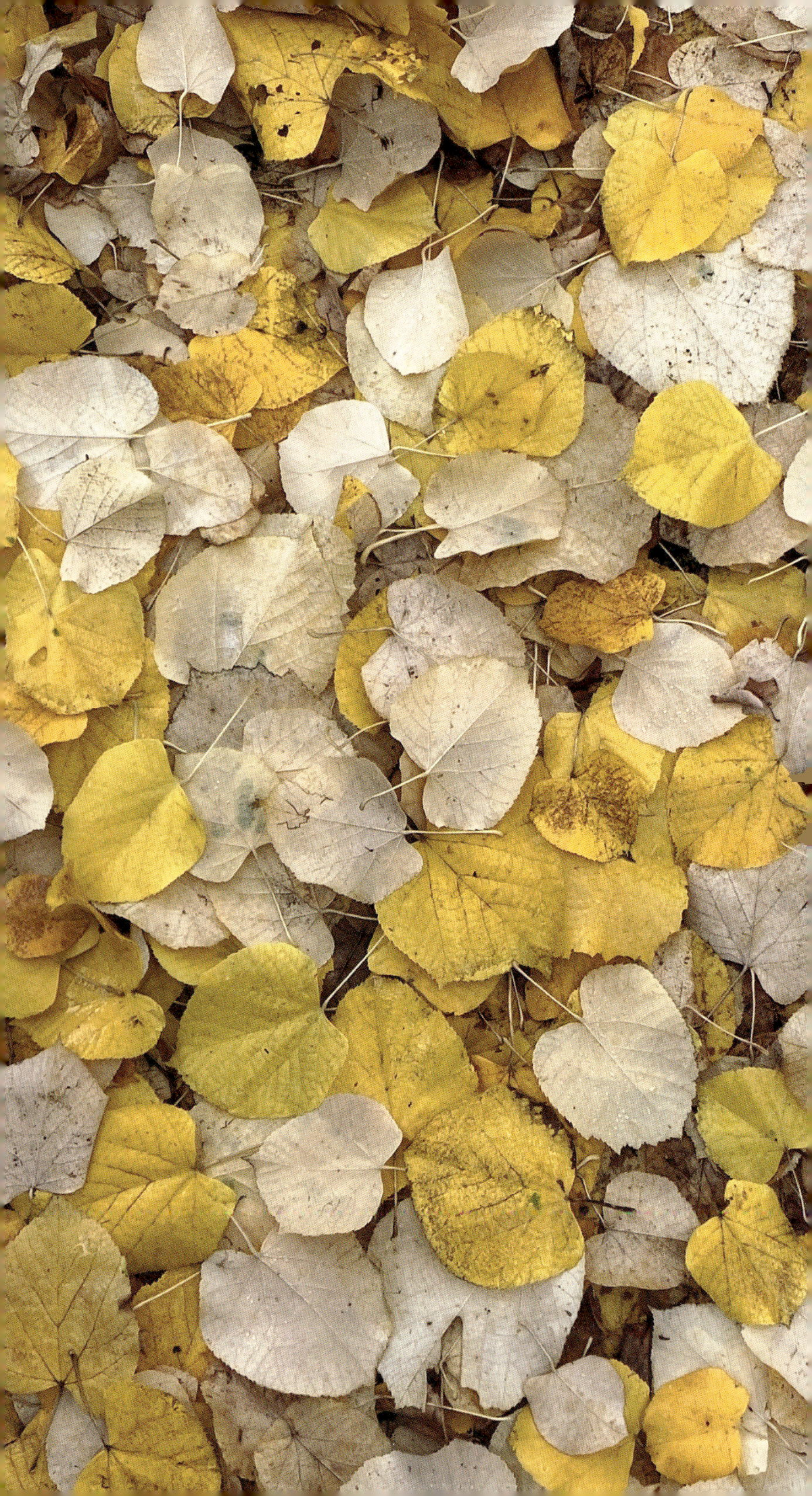

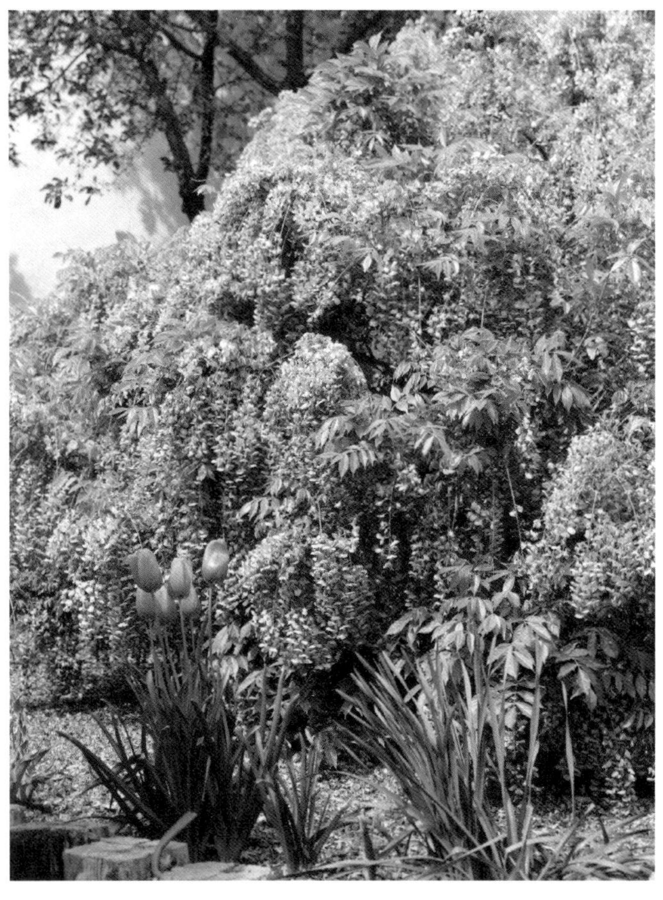

Artwork by Magali Duzant
unless otherwise indicated.

# ARTWORK CREDITS

1   **Palm on Plane**, 2023.

6   **Fifth Avenue III**, 2022.

10   **Nightwalk**, 2021.

16   **Ginkgo I**, 1968.
New York Public Library
Picture Collection.

18   **Blue and Yellow**, 1959.
New York Public Library
Picture Collection.

22   **Acorn**, 1975.
New York Public Library
Picture Collection.

24   **Baum (Zürich)**, 2022.

28   **Tulip Flower**, 1935.
New York Public Library
Picture Collection.

31   **The Queens Giant**, 2020.

34   **Black White Green**, 2021.

36   **Orange tree, loaded with
fruit, flowers, and buds**,
1850–1930. Stereograph.
The Miriam and Ira D. Wallach
Division of Art, Prints and
Photographs, New York
Public Library.

40   **Magnolia Shadow**, 2021.

43   **Cherry Blossom**, 2020.

46   **Caserta Laurel**, 2023.

52   **Wishing Tree**, 1936.
U.S. Works Progress
Administration.

55   **Tree of Hope**, 1941–1945.
Irma and Paul Milstein
Division of U.S. History,
Local History and Genealogy,
New York Public Library.

56   **Leaves and Flowers
(Ulmus serotina)**, 1956.
W.D. Brush, U.S. National
Archives.

60   **American Chestnut**, n.d.
Collotype. New York Public
Library Picture Collection.

62   **Weeping Beech Park**, 1942.
Irma and Paul Milstein
Division of U.S. History,
Local History and Genealogy,
New York Public Library.

66   **Xmas Tree**, 1910–1915.
Glass plate negative, 7x5in.
Bain News Service, Library of
Congress.

68   **Christmas Tree**, 1915.
Glass plate negative, 7x5in.
Raymond Dickey, Library of
Congress.

71   **August**, 2021.
Courtesy of Paul Brunner.

74   **Wisteria**, 2020.

79   **Dawn**, 2021.

80   **Flowering Dogwood**, 1931.
George B. Sudworth,
U.S. National Archives.

81   **Dogwood Blossom**, 1958.
George B. Sudworth,
U.S. National Archives.

82   **Ginkgo II**, 1968.
New York Public Library
Picture Collection.

83   **Autumn**, 1979.
New York Public Library
Picture Collection.

84   **Linden**, 2021.
Collage, 13x11in.

86   **Tree Hugger**, 1940.
Silver gelatin print.
Library of Congress.

87   **Acorn**, 1975.
New York Public Library
Picture Collection.

89   **Oak**, 2021.
Collage, 14x11in.

90   **Tulip Flower**, 1935.
New York Public Library
Picture Collection.

91   **Tulip Tree**, 1963.
New York Public Library
Picture Collection.

# ARTWORK CREDITS

93  **Yellow Poplar**, 2022.
Collage, 10x7.5in.

94  **Timber Related Crops**, 1933.
U.S. Forest Service and
the U.S. National Archives.

95  **After a Storm (Forest Park, Queens)**, 2020.

96  **Florida Palm I**, 2022.
Collage, 10x7.5in.

99  **Florida Palm II**, 2022.
Collage, 10x7.5in.

100  **Night Blossoms**, 2022.

101  **Blue Magnolia**, 2022.

102  **Bloom of Southern Magnolia**, 2021.
George B. Sudworth,
U.S. National Archives.

103  **Leaves and Fruit of California Laurel**, 1927.
Glass plate negative.
E.H. Morton, U.S. National
Archives.

104  **Apples**, 2022.

105  **Laurel Wreath**, 2023.

106  **California Laurel**, 1966.
U.S. National Archives.

107  **Fruit of Ulmus americana**,
1952. W.D. Brush, U.S.
National Archives.

108  **American Elm (Ulmus americana)**, 1938. W.G.
Baxter, U.S. National Archives.

109  **Herbarium Page (Ulmus americana)**, 1885/2019.
Collected by Frederick V.
Coville, Smithsonian
Institution Open Access.

110  **Morse Elm**, 1921.
Glass plate negative, 5x7in.
Library of Congress.

111  **People stand beside trees and a car**, 1920–1930.
Silver gelatin dry plate, 7x5in.
Tudor Washington Collins,
Auckland Museum.

113  **American Chestnut**, 2022.
Collage, 10x7.5in.

114  **Chestnut**, 1915.
Photogravure, 10x7.5in.
The Mentor Association,
New York Public Library
Picture Collection.

115  **Herbarium Page (Chestnut Blight)**, 1959/2019, Herbert F.
Darling, Smithsonian Institute
Open Access

116  **Xmas Tree, Madison Sq.**,
1910–1920. Glass plate
negative, 7x5in. Bain News
Service, Library of Congress.

117  **Weihnachten**, 2021.

118  **Linden, Yellow**, 2022.

119  **Woodhaven**, 2023.

120  **Spring Wisteria**, 1980–2006.
Transparency, 5x4in.
Carol M. Highsmith Archive,
[reproduction number, e.g.,
LC-USZ62-123456]. Prints
and Photographs Division,
Library of Congress. Digital
image produced by the artist
to represent her original film
transparency; some details
may differ between the film
and the digital images.

124  **Fifth Avenue III**, 2022.

128  **Sycamore**, 2021.

*Flowering Dogwood*
CORNUS FLORIDA

9–14

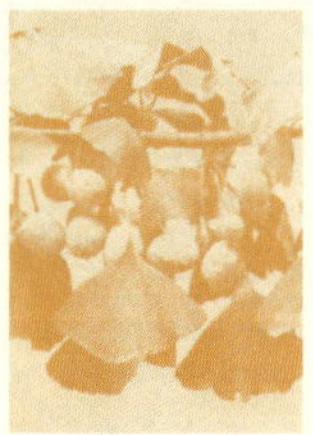

*Ginkgo*
GINKGO BILOBA

15–20

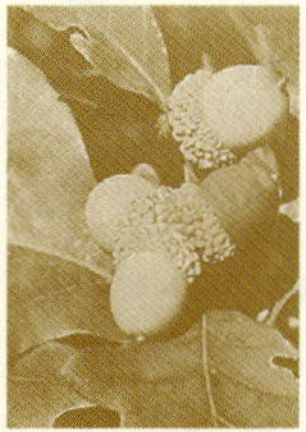

*Oak*
QUERCUS

*Linden*
TILIA

*Cypress*
CUPRESSUS

21–26

*Tulip Poplar*
LIRIODENDRON TULIPIFERA

27–32

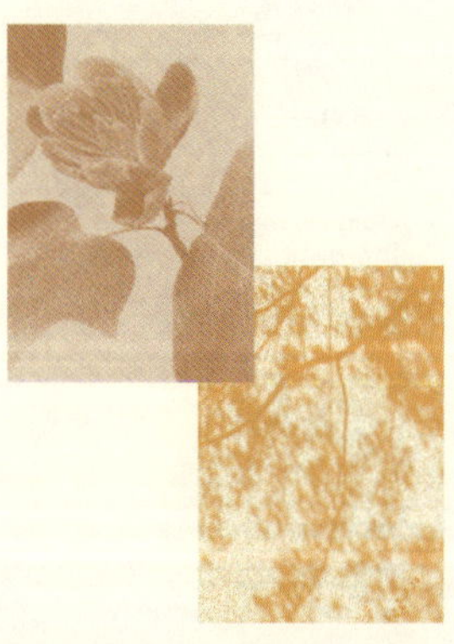

*Palm Tree*
ARECACEAE

*Sweet Orange*
CITRUS SINENSIS

33–38

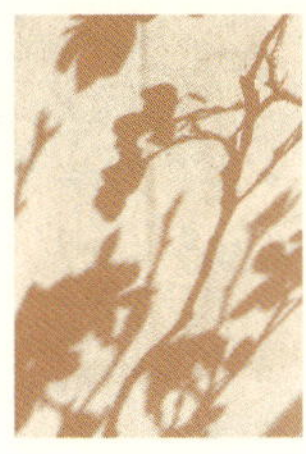

## Southern Magnolia
MAGNOLIA GRANDIFLORA

39–44

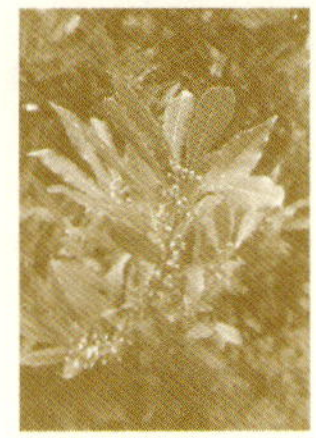

## Bay Laurel
LAURUS NOBILIS

45–50

## American Elm
ULMUS AMERICANA

51–58

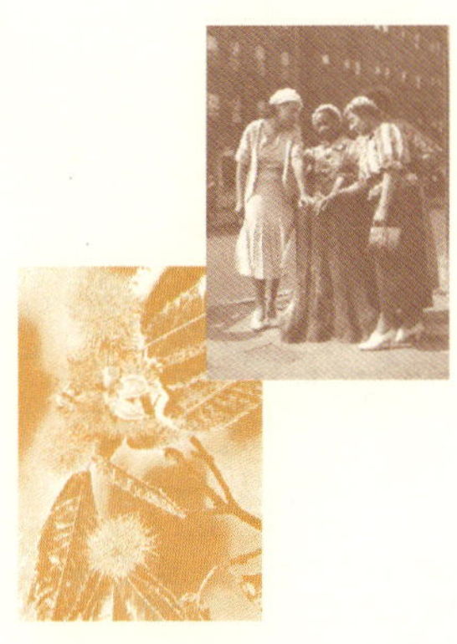

## American Chestnut
CASTANEA DENTATA

## Weeping Beech
FAGUS SYLVATICA 'PENDULA'

59–64

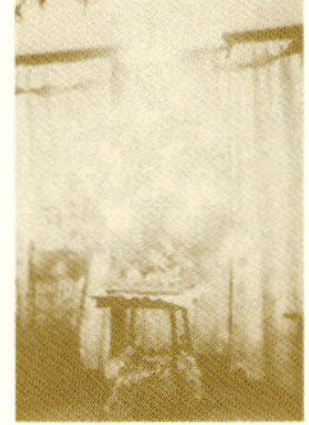

## Fir Tree
ABIES

65–72

## American Wisteria
WISTERIA FRUTESCENS

73–76